Praise for *Destination: Success!*

"This book provides a fascinating perspective on how to achieve the very best of you, and how you can inspire others to do so as well."

MELISSA REIFF
CEO, The Container Store

"This book is chock full of lessons to help you become the person you want to be. The lessons taught in *Destination: Success!* are a great personal investment. It has maximum impact when shared with employees and families!"

AL CLARK
Top State Farm Insurance Agent 19 years in a row

"Everyone wants the secret sauce – that one thing to help us gain faster traction toward our aspirations. *Destination: Success!* makes it clear there are many paths to follow, many ideas to consider and many people to help you along the way. I will have this book handy for reflection and inspiration."

VALERIE SOKOLOSKY
Fox News Contributor, Author of *Doing it Right*

"*Destination: Success!* is a precious gift. This book provides you with the tools and inspiration to become your very best. I encourage you to make the choice to be someone who permits others the opportunity to help you achieve success. Read this book and make that choice!"

LARRY SHAFFER
Senior Vice President of Marketing, Insperity

"A wonderful fable that teaches how to achieve success and how to share your wisdom with others. Implementing the lessons taught in *Destination: Success!* will help you become the person you want to be."

MARSHALL GOLDSMITH
Thinkers 50 #1 Executive Coach for 10 years

Destination:
SUCCESS!

Other Books by David Cottrell

Becoming the Obvious Choice: A guide to your next opportunity

Birdies, Pars, and Bogeys: Leadership Lessons from the Links

Escape from Management Land: A journey every team wants their manager to take

Grace Upon Grace: My story.

Indispensable! Becoming the Obvious Choice in Business and in Life

Listen Up, Leader

LeaderShift: Making Leadership Everyone's Business

Leadership ... Biblically Speaking: The power of principle-based leadership

Monday Morning Choices: 12 Powerful Ways to Go from Everyday to Extraordinary

Monday Morning Customer Service:

Monday Morning Leadership: 8 Mentoring Sessions You Can't Afford to Miss

Monday Morning Leadership for Kids

Monday Morning Mentoring: Ten Lessons to Guide You Up the Ladder

Monday Morning Motivation: Five steps to energize your team, customers, and profits

Second Quarter: Get the Most Out of Life's Toughest Times

The First Two Rules of Leadership: Don't be Stupid. Don't be a Jerk.

The Magic Question: A simple question every leader dreams of answering

The Nature of Excellence

The Next Level: Leading beyond the status quo

Time! 105 Ways to Get More Done Every Workday

Tuesday Morning Coaching: Eight Simple Truths to Boost Your Career and Your Life

Winners Always Quit! Seven Pretty Good Habits You Can Swap for Really Great Results

Destination:
SUCCESS !

Chart your course
to achieve your best

David Cottrell

Destination:
SUCCESS!

Chart your course
to achieve your best

CornerStone Leadership Institute
P.O. Box 764087
Dallas, TX 75376
972-298-8377

ISBN: 978-0-9600155-2-8
Printed in the United States of America. 10 9 8 7 6 5 4 3 2

Credits
Copy editors: Brenda Quinn
                                                          Alice Adams

Design, art direction, and production: Melissa Farr, Back Porch Creative,
                                                          info@backporchcreative.com

Contents

Jack Davis' Journey

Jack Davis was a lot like you and me.

He was doing okay. He worked hard and was a good person. He had thrived during the early stages of his career, but now he was just "getting by." He'd always thought of himself as confident, bold and driven – but lately he wondered if that was truly who he was. His self-esteem was a mere shadow of what it had been in the past, and every day it seemed that the success he wanted was slipping further away.

The worst part was that the more Jack thought that way, the more that seemed to be the truth.

His lack of growth at work added unrelated frustrations at home. He was happily married but his home life had become dull and routine. He wasn't making much progress at work or at home. His dream of success and happiness was slowly evading him.

Jack was not becoming the person he wanted to be. He was stuck and he was dissatisfied. He wanted more for himself and his family and he knew he could do better.

On his way home from work one day, he heard a podcaster express her views about the secrets to success. One of the host's opinions was that there is no 'self-made' success. Few people, if any, had achieved success without the help of others. The successful people the podcaster host interviewed on her show talked about mentors who had helped guide them by sharing their experience, knowledge, passion and wisdom. They all said that without the mentors' assistance, their success would have probably never happened.

Jack listened, then questioned out loud: "Who are these people? Where can I find them? Is there anyone out there who would be willing to guide *me*? If I'm ever going to become the person I want to be, I need to find someone – a mentor – who will help me."

Thus, Jack's journey began.

This is Jack's story.

1

Blast Through Tough

Jack decided he'd start his journey by searching for successful people. He wanted to learn how they had achieved their success. He wanted to know what they'd done that was different from what he'd done and what was unique to their approach.

He began his quest by asking his friends, neighbors and work associates: "Who is the most successful person you know?" Several people were recommended to him but one person who was consistently mentioned was a guy named Vince Garrett. Vince was the CEO of a regional hospital network. He was one of the most respected people in his town, and also known as one of the most philanthropic.

Jack debated within himself. *Should he call a stranger and ask for advice?* His pride said no, but his reality said why not? He had nothing to lose.

After he decided to reach out to Vince, it was a couple of weeks before he mustered the courage to actually make the call. He and Vince exchanged several messages before they connected. When Jack finally talked to Vince, he was so nervous that he had to keep referring to the notes he'd written for himself. He briefly explained his situation and told Vince he was willing to do whatever was necessary to move forward and start to become the person he wanted to be.

Vince listened to Jack's request, asked a few questions and then graciously agreed to meet with Jack for a few minutes the following Monday morning.

On Monday, Jack left his home for the thirty-minute drive to Vince's office. On the way, he became upset with himself that he had to ask for help to get his career and life back on track. "This is humiliating," he muttered. "I'm just wasting my time and Vince's time." For several minutes he chastised himself and nearly turned around to head home. But he soon calmed down and realized that this meeting with Vince was probably necessary. He was stuck and needed help.

Jack arrived at Vince's office just as Vince was completing a draft of a speech he was scheduled to deliver at a National Association of Business Leaders convention. He immediately closed his notebook and welcomed Jack. Vince's voice was soft but businesslike. His smile was so broad that Jack couldn't help but feel at ease, and he noticed that Vince's eyes were focused intently on him. His initial impression of Vince was that he was a kind, compassionate and successful person.

Before taking their seats around a small table, Vince offered Jack a cup of coffee. Jack poured his cup and then nervously overloaded it with sugar and cream, filling his cup to the brim.

Embarrassed, he carefully drank the thick, tan mix as quickly as he could get it down.

After the two men spent a few minutes in ice-breaking conversation and laughing about the coffee mishap, Vince loosened his tie, which hung from a perfect half Windsor knot over a neatly pressed shirt. "How can I help?" he began.

"Thanks for meeting with me," Jack said, then paused to clear his throat. "You were recommended to me by several people as someone who'd be willing to share the story behind your success. As I mentioned on the phone, I'm struggling in my career. I feel like I'm stuck and can't seem to find my way out. I'm searching for successful people who I can learn from and begin moving forward again. I called you because I want to learn from you. Could you maybe provide some words of wisdom, or tell me about a particular principle that guided you toward your success?"

Vince took a sip of coffee from his mug and smiled to himself before responding to Jack's question. "First, I want to thank you for asking my opinion. I can definitely relate to your situation. I have been exactly where you are right now. It took courage for you to call. Many people will make a decision to do something to improve their situation but fail to do anything about it. Making a decision without taking action is worthless. I'm glad my name was given to you and you made the call." He smiled warmly, and Jack felt reassured.

"At one time or another, everyone has to identify and address the shocking gap between what they expected from their career or life and the reality of what they are experiencing. This may be inconceivable to you right now, but some things are learned best while going through a disappointing time."

Jack nodded in reply and Vince continued. "Even though it's taken us a little time to get together, one thing I already admire about you is that you didn't give up on pursuing this meeting. Your perseverance and determination are great qualities. I am glad that we were able to find a time that worked for both of us."

"I know your time is valuable," Jack acknowledged. "Sitting down with you is important to me, and I was willing to do whatever it took to meet with you."

"Well," Vince leaned back in his chair. "I'm definitely flattered. The question you asked doesn't have an easy answer … one principle that has meant the most to my success?" He paused before he continued. "I believe every person needs to discover their own personal keys to success, which involves being great at several things that are independent yet connected. It's not a spur-of-the-moment, unrehearsed event; success is a process with peaks and valleys along the way.

"The situation you describe – the disappointments, the struggle, the need for help – is not unusual. One of the keys to getting back on track is to not overreact. When you're frustrated, everything tends to seem worse than it really is. It's not a good time to jump ship or make dramatic decisions. However, it's also not the time to just sit there and hope things magically improve, either."

"I know," Jack said. "And that's why I'm glad I'm here."

Vince resumed, keeping his focus on Jack. "It's good you're seeking advice. Many successful people have been where you are and have worked their way through a tough time. In fact, everyone is either in, coming out of, or headed toward a tough time – those are just a part of life. This meeting today can be the first step in getting unstuck and becoming the person you want to be."

"I certainly hope so." Jack thought for a moment, his index finger tracing the rim of his coffee cup. "It's taken me a while to get to the point of seeking advice and counsel. As you may have gathered, I'm not great at admitting I need some help."

"Not many people are," Vince said with a smile. "I wish I could wave a magic wand to improve your situation – but if I did, you might not appreciate the journey you're embarking on."

Appreciate this journey? Jack said to himself. *I can't even imagine that.* But he knew Vince's advice came from experience, so he nodded and smiled.

"It's important you accept that there is no grand conspiracy preventing you from achieving success," Vince continued. "The success game is not rigged so that some people have all the advantages and succeed, and others have all the disadvantages and fail. I doubt anyone is sitting around scheming up ways to make your life miserable. The challenges you face are not there to destroy you; they are there to re-direct you to the path that's right for you.

"Instead of thinking like a victim and asking yourself, 'Why is this happening to me?', ask yourself, 'What is this trying to teach me?' Once you accept the fact that you're not a victim, your success journey can begin. You will reach your definition of success only when you understand and build upon your unique talents."

Jack chuckled self-consciously. "So how do I find out what my talents are? I don't see much to brag about. There's not a lot of good stuff going on in my life right now."

"Yes, if things were going great, we would probably not be sitting here." Vince's voice softened, and he appeared to genuinely want to help. "Just remember – your *situation* is not unique. There are many people who don't know where they are especially gifted. But *you* are unique because you're asking, questioning, searching to find out for yourself how you can become the person you want to be. Your journey will lead you to the discovery of your talents ... you just wait and see."

Vince allowed those words to sink in before continuing. "I believe to achieve success – however you define it – you first have to feel great about yourself. Your self-esteem should not fluctuate based on your most recent or next decision. And it shouldn't be based on the economy, stock market performance, weather or anything else that is beyond your control.

"You can't expect others to feel great about you if you don't feel great about yourself. Your job performance, as well as your home life, is a reflection of your own self-image. It's difficult – almost impossible – to be great, either personally or professionally, when you don't feel great about yourself. I'm glad you came to see me, but your success journey really begins with the reflection in your mirror. That may be the best advice I give you."

"I'm glad I came too," said Jack, nodding. "And yes, I see what you're saying."

Vince continued. "However, my answer to your question about the principle that has served me best is simply this: *I blast through tough*. Regardless of what happens along the way, I will do whatever it takes to keep moving forward when things get tough."

"What do you mean? How do you blast through tough?" Jack wanted to know.

"I found the best way to move toward a positive future is for me to take an active part in guiding it," Vince replied. "That meant I had to accept total responsibility – without blaming, complaining or making excuses. If I didn't like the results I was achieving, I first had to check my own behavior. Then, I had to quit complaining about bad luck or being in a bad situation.

"I had to take ownership of my thoughts and actions," he said, "and that was hard for me to accept. But when I looked around, the blaming was not helping anything. Actually, blaming others took away my power to change things. The excuses didn't improve my confidence, and my complaining was mostly to someone who couldn't do anything to fix what I was complaining about. And the grim reality was that most people didn't care about my problems. It also surprised me that many of those who *did* care were sort of glad I had them. Very seldom, if ever, did my blaming, complaining, or excuse-making do any good. In fact, it was a waste of my time, emotions and energy."

"I can relate to that," Jack confessed. "I'll admit, I've also fallen into the blaming, complaining, and excuses trap. I don't enjoy it, but it seems everyone around me is also in the blaming, complaining, and excuses trap. And, quite frankly, there's not a lot going on that is positive, so it's easy to get caught up in the negativity."

"I understand," Vince was quick to respond. "Very little that's worthwhile comes easy. Somewhere along the way, something or someone will get in your way, impeding your progress.

Then you'll have to make a decision to retreat or blast through the tough situation.

"Remember, Jack, that your success and happiness will ultimately be molded by your decisions, not by some temporary conditions. Closing the gap of who you are and who you want to be is dependent on what you do. You make your choices, and then your choices will make you. Your situation may be unfair, and you may never understand why it's happening to you. Regardless, you do have a choice in how you respond – you either blast through it or yield to it. If you don't take control, your negative situation will literally consume your thoughts, actions and enthusiasm, and as it consumes you, it will rob you of your ability to move forward."

Vince paused before continuing. "You're facing a life-changing moment right here, right now. Be thankful for it."

Jack squirmed uncomfortably before admitting the cold, hard facts of his situation. "Well, I assure you, I am not thankful that my career and life are in the stuck mode. I don't think I should be where I am, and it's humiliating that I'm even sitting here, sharing my problems with you."

Vince wasn't alarmed at Jack's explanation. "It may be humiliating, but you took a major step forward today when you walked through my office door. Most people are surprised when *tough* pops up, but there's no reason to be surprised. *Tough* eventually shows up for everyone. You have to hang in there and figure out how to move forward."

"So," Jack interjected, "you're recommending I hang in there. Will 'hanging in there' help blast me through tough?"

"Let me clarify that," Vince said quickly. "Unfortunately, it's not that simple. Hanging in there too long could lead to failure, as well.

"It's similar to hanging onto a rope. When you are rappelling a mountain, to make progress, you have to *hang onto* the rope with all the strength you can muster. Letting go would be catastrophic. However, suppose you're water skiing and you lose your balance. You continue to hang on to the ski rope and are thrown all over the place. In that instance, if you don't *let go* of the rope, the water will beat you to death. My point, of course, is you have to know when to hang on and when to let go."

"But how do I know?" Jack questioned. "You said sometimes I need to hang on and sometimes I need to let go. Tell me, how will I know what to do?"

Jack's expression prompted Vince's careful response. "That's a fair question. Your answer should contain equal doses of faith and reason. You first have to have **faith** you are pursuing the right thing for you at this juncture of your life. Then, it has to pass the **reasonable** test.

"When you reach your life-changing moment, you may only want to listen to yourself … and you will likely only hear what you want to hear."

Jack noticed that Vince's voice became more serious and his gaze more penetrating. Vince leaned forward. "Listen closely. Your faith needs to be verified by your mentors and trusted advisors. When you talk to them about your plan, they'll help you determine if it's reasonable. More importantly, they will make you accountable for how you will measure success."

"I have several friends who have been providing advice," Jack said proudly. "They want to help me. I feel pretty good about them being my advisors."

"I understand how you feel about your friends' advice," Vince said slowly. "But let me offer a different perspective. Speaking from my own experiences and my observations of many others, close friends do not provide great advice. They want you to follow your dream, so they don't want to hurt your feelings. Your advisors are critically important … they can make or break you. I strongly believe that the best advisors are professional acquaintances, people who have more experience than you, and who will tell you the truth from their perspective, even if it hurts your feelings. Without bias, they will confirm your faith to move forward or provide a practical reason for you to let go."

"Yeah, but…," Jack countered. "But what if my situation is not as clear as yes or no?"

"Your advisors will help you discern whether or not your goals are realistic," Vince continued. "If your well-thought-out answer is to stay the course, then go full speed ahead. If your answer is to let go of the dream, have the courage to make that decision. Just don't straddle the fence.

"Most of the time, people don't quit because their journey is unreasonable or unrealistic. They give up because they get impatient. They quit because the journey is tough," Vince emphasized. "Once you make the decision to move forward, you have to blast through tough, pull yourself up, avoid the 'why' trap and design your next move forward. Regardless of how bleak the situation appears, you have to keep moving. Don't quit. Don't panic. Saddle up. Keep moving. Begin blasting."

"Yeah," Jack said. "I guess I need to work on developing a 'blast through tough' attitude if I want to succeed."

"Having a 'blast through tough' attitude does not guarantee success," Vince continued. "It just reminds you to not even think about quitting when your journey gets tough. People who quit lose that opportunity. You have to keep moving. Spending your energy complaining, justifying, and blaming others changes nothing. It just drains away the energy you'll need to blast through your situation.

"Also, if you're like most, you'll be tempted to take shortcuts. Be careful of shortcuts. Believe it or not, most of the time the shortcuts become much longer routes."

Jack nodded. "I can relate to that," he said. "I've taken shortcuts that led me back to the starting line more often than I want to admit."

Vince's assistant entered his office and announced that his next appointment had arrived.

"I'd love to continue our conversation, Jack, but I have other meetings scheduled," Vince said. "Let me emphasize that there are no silver bullets or scratch-and-win moves that will catapult you to unimaginable success. Successful people are not simply extraordinary people whom fate smiled on and then boom! … they magically achieved their goals. No, successful people followed a plan that led them to their success. In every instance that I know of, success did not happen alone or overnight. It took years to achieve and required the help of others.

"You're off to a good start, Jack. You may have heard the saying that 'nothing changes if nothing changes.' You've made your first move, now things can begin changing for the better. It's up to you to take control of your situation, right now, right where you are."

Vince stood up and smiled warmly. "If you don't mind me asking, where are you going from here?"

"I'm not sure," Jack sheepishly replied. "You were my first visit and I wasn't sure how this would work. Sharing my issues with you was humiliating, but I'm glad I did it. There's one thing I want to clarify. Earlier you said I should be thankful for my situation. How can I be thankful for being stuck in neutral?"

Vince smiled before answering. "You'll find out on your own. I'll bet your very best is ahead of you. And you'll realize that without blasting through the tough time you're now facing, you would never have reached your potential. Wait and see."

"I hope so." Jack was skeptical, but Vince's positive tone was encouraging. "I don't feel too great about where I am right now, but I assure you I'm going to give it my best shot. In fact, I'm going to make a few 'Blast Through Tough' note cards and place one on the back of my phone, on my desk and in my car. Almost everywhere I go, a 'Blast Through Tough' reminder will be in sight."

Vince seemed pleased. "Great idea! The reminders will prompt you to remember that regardless of the situation you're facing, you can make it through. I also recommend that you continue gathering information from other successful people. When you do, make sure you leave with several action items from the conversation. You can use those actions to begin building your own success plan."

Jack smiled broadly for the first time. "I will. I have several action items that surfaced in our conversation. I appreciate your encouragement and the time that you've taken to visit with me."

Then he asked a question he had been reluctant to ask earlier: "Is there someone you recommend I talk to?"

Vince thought for a few seconds and then was happy to recommend another mentor. "Most people love to tell their story. Maybe you should call a friend of mine, Ashley Pearce. Ask her if she'll share her success secrets. Here's her number," he said, writing a phone number on a notepad. "Tell her I suggested that you call."

"I will," Jack said. "I see Ashley occasionally, but I've always been uncomfortable around her so I've never actually spoken to her. Maybe a meeting will help me understand her better. Thanks for your time," he said as they shook hands. "You've given me insight I could not have learned on my own, or from my friends. I'll keep you updated on my progress."

Jack left Vince's office with mixed feelings. He was still disappointed in himself for his current situation but pleased that he'd called Vince for advice. He had taken his first step on his journey.

Vince's Lessons:

Success will not arrive as one great, spontaneous event. It will be a combination of several factors that are interdependently connected.

I need mentors – people outside my normal circle of friends.

My performance reflects my self-image. I have to feel great about myself.

There is no grand conspiracy preventing me from success. I must take total ownership of my success without complaining, blaming or making excuses.

Most of the time, shortcuts become the longest routes.

I will blast through tough and keep moving.

2

Hug Change

Ashley Pearce was well known in Jack's community. Many people thought of her as a loner. She was a successful chief marketing officer for a large organization, but she was unique. Her demeanor was confident – confident enough to try new and unusual things.

Ashley was definitely not like everyone else.

Vince had told her to expect Jack's call and after one phone call the meeting was set. Even though he only knew her by reputation, Jack was eager to hear the story behind her success.

When Jack arrived at Ashley's office, she seemed happy to meet with him. After settling into their comfortable chairs, several minutes of uneasy and difficult rapport-building followed. But Jack realized Ashley wasn't as intimidating as she'd once seemed, so he felt comfortable enough to ask her his question: "Is there one important principle you believe has contributed the most to your success?"

Ashley reflected for a moment and then answered. "I haven't been asked that question in a long time … maybe ever. I tend to look at things contrarily to most people. They rarely take the time to understand me. I appreciate your asking.

"If I had to boil down all the elements to one principle that has helped me, it would be that I enjoy the process of change. In fact, I believe that you should *hug change*. That may be one of the reasons people see me as different from most. I don't enjoy change just for the sake of change, but I love the improvement that can only emerge after a change has been made."

Jack was astonished. "You are the first person I've ever met who said they enjoyed change. Most people I know hate change."

"That's not surprising," Ashley agreed, "and I believe you. So, why do you think change is such a dreaded undertaking for so many people?"

Jack thought for a few seconds. "Change is hard. It requires you to break out of the ordinary. Most people are comfortable with keeping things as they are."

Ashley nodded her agreement, then added, "I think change is usually resisted because people are trapped by their own perspective. In reality, everyone is limited by their experiences and 'data points.' For instance, if you were raised in a military family, your perception of normal is based on the experiences you had growing up. If you were raised in a small rural town, your data points are small-town experiences. If you were raised in a large urban city, your opinions are formed by completely different data points. You also have data points based on the size of your family and your place in it, such as oldest, middle child, etc., as well as the gender of family members, religion, ethnicity, and significant personal events that molded your thinking. In most cases, your beliefs and ideas are generated from a small sample size of people whose experiences are similar to yours.

"When a change comes along, new and different data points are introduced. A perfectly natural reaction to change is intimidation. The unknown can be scary. You may also feel vulnerable, based on your lack of control or understanding of the new situation."

Jack pondered Ashley's words. "So, if everyone is framed by their own data points, any change will affect everyone differently? Hmm. That makes hugging change even more difficult, especially if there isn't a crisis and some people may not see the need for any change at all."

"Exactly. A lot of people look at me as though I'm crazy when I suggest changing something that doesn't appear to be completely broken," Ashley shared. "They don't understand. I am not trying to break it; I'm trying to improve it so that we can be more successful. The way I see it, if you want long-term success, adjustments are necessary and unavoidable. You have to continually make changes."

"That is unusual," Jack said, almost thinking out loud. "Most people would say that if it's not broken, don't fix it. In fact, I believe that as well. Why should you waste time repairing something that's not broken when there are probably plenty of other things that need fixing?"

"I've heard others make the same point many times." Ashley paused, seeming to savor the moment before continuing. "That's a popular stance. I even agree that most of the time, there are other things that need to be fixed.

"However, regardless of what you attempt to fix, some people – usually the same people – will be opposed to any change, even a change that obviously improves their current situation. In fact, I anticipate irrational responses to any change because it will be accompanied by emotional reactions. Being a change resister instead of a change hugger is, unfortunately, human nature."

Ashley paused before continuing. "A question I love to hear is, 'What would happen if?' That simple question exposes possibilities. If you look at some traditional industries, you'll find many of the current leaders in those industries weren't taken seriously when they started, and in fact, they weren't even considered to be in the business in which they now flourish. Uber and Lyft are transportation companies that don't own vehicles. Airbnb is a leader in the hospitality sector and yet they don't own hotels. Facebook is a media leader that doesn't utilize traditional media outlets. Before those organizations began, someone had to ask, 'What would happen if?'"

Jack acknowledged, "Those organizations certainly disrupted their industries. I guess all great companies began with someone asking, 'What would happen if.'"

"You're absolutely right," Ashley nodded. "And successful individuals ask the same question of themselves. But they add one word: What would happen if *I* ..."

"I guess you're right," Jack responded. "Everyone has to change something to reach their next level of success. However, I think most people are like me and look to change only when they're desperate."

Ashley was definitely in her element. "For sure, your reaction is the same as most people's. But change should be hugged and welcomed, even when things are going well. John F. Kennedy once said, 'The time to repair the roof is when the sun is shining.' There is a lot of wisdom in such a simple statement. It's foolish to wait until a hailstorm approaches to repair the roof. However, many people won't even think about their roof until the rain is dripping on their sofa and flooding the floors. Then, they *have* to repair the roof, the sofa and the carpet. They would rather do anything else than change … even if a disaster is coming."

Then abruptly, Ashley changed the subject. "Do you remember reading a book in high school – *The Road Less Traveled?*"

"I don't remember that one," Jack laughed. "I must have been sick that day."

"Right," Ashley laughed with him. "If you had been there, you would have found out that the road the author wrote about had a sign at the entrance that read, 'Life is difficult.' In fact, those three words were centered on the first page of the book.

"The reason that road was less traveled was because it was difficult. People would pass it by because they were looking for Easy Street – the road without difficulties. But, as we all eventually learn, there is no Easy Street. Traveling on what you think is Easy Street will lead to doing the same things over and over.

"It's easy to become content with the status quo because it's comfortable. But you cannot improve while you are doing the same things over and over. Eventually, you have to make the decision to get out of your comfortable rut and do things differently."

"You're right," said Jack, jumping into the conversation. "You've just described exactly where I am. I was comfortable, but today I find myself stuck in a rut. So now I'm trying to figure out what I need to change so I can start moving forward again."

Ashley continued. "It takes a lot of courage to recognize that you need to make changes. Courage is facing and dealing with anything dangerous, difficult or painful instead of withdrawing from it. That sounds a whole lot like change, doesn't it?"

"I had never connected courage to change," Jack answered. "But that's exactly what I see right now – difficulty and pain with the changes I need to make. No one enjoys pain, so I guess that courage and change must go hand in hand."

"They do," Ashley chimed in. "Change is not going away, and it takes courage to make changes. Now, I'm going to test you again," she warned. "Have you ever heard the phrase, 'The only constant is change?'"

Jack thought for a moment and smiled wryly. "I first heard it a long time ago … and I've heard it many times since then. Now that I think about it, maybe it was on the test after that class I missed on *The Road Less Traveled*."

"That was an important class that you missed," Ashley smiled.

Jack was pleasantly surprised to discover that Ashley had a sense of humor. He'd often heard that she was unusual, but he was beginning to like her.

"When do you think that phrase first appeared?" Ashley asked. "Was it last year … two years ago … thirty years ago…?"

Jack thought for a moment. "Well, I'm not sure when, but it's been around for a while. I would say Ben Franklin probably came up with it."

"Good guess, but you're about 2,000 years off," Ashley remarked sarcastically, still smiling. "Actually, Heraclitus was the first person credited with saying, 'The only constant is change' in 500 BC, and even he probably didn't make it up. I wouldn't be surprised if he saw it on the side of a cave wall somewhere and put his name under it."

"But he could not have been envisioning the type of changes we face today," Jack said, turning serious.

"Probably not," Ashley said quickly. "Nevertheless, almost 2,000 years ago accepting change undoubtedly came with its own unique challenges. Then and now, everyone resists change in varying degrees. Even the smallest of changes is naturally resisted. Clearly, the message of Heraclitus 2,000 years ago is that change is here to stay."

Ashley paused before continuing. "Change is a good thing. You can't improve without changing something. Change is as natural as breathing, yet many seem to prefer taking their last breath rather than change – even if it's required for survival.

"So, since things will definitely change, why not hug it when it shows up? I've seen people hunker down, refuse to change and wind up losing everything. They become complacent, content, unwilling to change. They keep trying to 'saw sawdust,' at the risk of losing everything.

"Then there are some who refuse to accept that there's a risk in doing nothing. The truth is, complacency is the root of mediocrity. And mediocrity is success's worst enemy – it's a greater enemy than failure. Failure can lead to success because it forces you to move in a different direction. Mediocrity, on the other hand, prevents success because it keeps you comfortable, nestled into the status quo."

Ashley's tone was serious. "You must let go to grow. That's the beginning of progress. Change should be embraced and hugged without fear. It allows you to move forward and look to the future with confidence."

Something about Ashley's theory was gnawing at Jack. "I hear what you're saying, and I don't disagree in theory. But change is tough – sometimes really tough – for everyone."

"Change *is* tough," Ashley acknowledged, nodding slowly. "Most people prefer stability and comfort. Change typically represents the opposite – discomfort and instability – and very few people enjoy traveling into those regions."

Ashley let that sink in for a moment before continuing. "I've learned that if I want other people to hug a change that I suggest, I have to seek out the perspective of those who have opinions opposed to mine. It's easy to listen to people who have opinions identical to mine. But if I do that, I'm limiting data points that will help me see things differently and make a better-informed decision. You may not agree with those people who think differently from you, and their views may not alter your perspective. But listening to differing opinions provides you additional information before you hug your change and ask others to hug it with you.

"There are a couple of important lessons that I've learned about hugging change. First, when a change comes along, go with it. Don't wait and hope that things will return to the way they were in the past. You must accept that things are always going to change, and improvement will not mysteriously appear on its own. You have to move with the change, or you'll probably find yourself trying to catch up with everyone else.

"Also, when things are going well, keep looking for things to improve. That's the best time to make positive changes. You can see more clearly and experience less stress because you're not in a panic mode. The best time to adjust is when things appear to be going just fine. Remember, fix the roof while the sun is shining."

Jack sat in silence, trying to calm himself. He refused to believe what Ashley was saying. "Really? What you're saying is so contrary to how most people think, it's difficult to grasp."

Ashley smiled impassively. She had obviously heard this before. "I hear you. I get it. However, there's a night-and-day difference between those who choose to proactively make changes and those who refuse to change. I'm not talking a ten, twenty, or even fifty percent difference. The difference in many cases is everything – success or failure.

"I mentioned earlier that change requires courage because you cannot make changes without having the courage to exit from where you are comfortable. I also think it's important and interesting to understand the relationship between courage and fear. What would you say is the opposite of courage?"

After reflecting, Jack was confident with his answer. "I think cowardice, or maybe fear, is the opposite of courage.'"

"Sure, both of those answers could apply," Ashley affirmed. "Some people say the opposite of courage is ignorance. Still others believe courage means not feeling fear at all. Mark Twain defined courage as 'resistance to fear, mastery of fear – but not absence of fear.' You walk forward along a path. Fear is there too, but you keep walking.

"I think the most appropriate answer is this: the opposite of courage is conformity. Courage is having the guts and the heart to do things differently for the sake of progress. Improvement doesn't happen by taking the path of least resistance or by conforming to the way things have always been."

Jack found himself intrigued with Ashley's perspective on change. It was beginning to make sense. "My resistance to change may have been one factor that put me in the situation I'm in. I need to work on hugging change."

Their time was up, but as Jack was about to leave, Ashley offered one last piece of advice. "Your success will not happen because of one belief, one attitude or one phrase. The most important principle for me has been to hug change, but others have a different perspective that's most important to them. You may want to visit with my colleague, Brad Harris. You'll probably discover another principle that's just as important to him as hugging change has been to me."

"I'll do that," Jack promised. "Thank you for pointing me in his direction."

As Jack exited Ashley's office, he reflected on her advice. Her outlook on change was indeed unique. He realized that every successful person he visited would generate new ideas and suggestions on what he needed to change.

Now it was time to change his own perspective. If he was going to become the person he wanted to be, he was going to have to hug change.

Ashley's Lessons:

I should welcome change, even when things are going well.

I need to increase my data points before I make a significant change.

I must let go to grow.

All improvement requires change. Improvement will not magically appear without something changing.

The opposite of courage is conformity.

An enemy to my growth is complacency.

I should not judge people who appear different or unusual to me.

3

Quit Drifting

Like Ashley, Brad Harris was well known in Jack's town. He'd enjoyed a long and successful career. Brad had led several organizations to success from the brink of failure, and was considered a turnaround expert. He seemed to always figure out a way to keep his cool and win, even in bad economic times. Most people agreed that he was laid back and easygoing, but he was also blessed with the gift of getting things done.

Jack and Brad ran in different circles and had never met. Their personalities were polar opposites: Jack was outgoing, competitive, hard charging, and impatient – a prototypical Type A. Brad was often described as cool, calm and collected – words that Jack barely knew, and had never heard said about him.

Jack was excited, yet a little uneasy when Brad agreed to meet with him and share his experiences. As the CEO of an influential organization, Brad's schedule was extremely busy, so it took several attempts to find a time that fit into his schedule. They finally agreed to meet at 5:30 p.m. on Tuesday afternoon.

Jack arrived at Brad's building and was escorted to his large, well-appointed office. It was immaculate. There was no clutter on his desk or any sign of chaos that is often associated with busy, successful leaders. In fact, Brad's office was the contrary; it gave the impression that everything was under control.

Brad's physical appearance reflected his calm demeanor – every hair was in its proper place, his suit looked custom made and his polished black shoes reflected the late afternoon sun beaming through his window. He looked impressive and successful.

When he stepped into Brad's office space, Jack noticed a plaque hanging on the wall. It had only two words: ***Quit Drifting!*** *Interesting*, he thought to himself.

Brad served on the board of directors for several organizations, had mentored numerous successful people, and was considered ultra-successful. Yet, there were no plaques, awards or any notable signs of success around his office. The only thing hanging on his wall was the simple inscription, Quit Drifting!

The two men exchanged pleasantries and settled comfortably into two plush hard-back mahogany chairs. Jack was slowly getting used to talking to leaders, and this time he realized the uneasiness he'd felt in his two previous appointments was gone.

Jack and Brad chatted amiably for a few minutes about their favorite college football teams, and he thanked Brad for taking the time to meet. "Before we begin, I must admit that your office is the most orderly workspace I've ever seen. How do you keep it like this?"

Brad smiled. "Ha. It's interesting that you noticed. My office was not always like this. Early in my career, even a little clutter would grow and eventually fill every inch of my desk. It drove me crazy. Now I make it a nightly ritual to clean my desk when I leave every evening. I despise clutter. It may seem a little strange but staring at a clean desk when I enter my office helps start my day a little better. Of course, my to-do list doesn't expand or contract based on how clean my desk is, but a clear workspace helps me focus on what is important at the time."

Jack was impressed. "I don't think it's strange, but it's quite different from my desk. Yours definitely looks a lot better. I've already learned something from you. I'm impressed and a little intimidated. You've given me something to think about."

Jack told Brad about his mission to learn the secret of success from influential people and added that Ashley Pearce had suggested they meet. "My main question for you is this: What guiding principle do you think has influenced your success the most?"

"Thanks for including me on your list," Brad humbly acknowledged. "To answer your question, there are many different factors that work together to help with any achievement. I'm not sure you can nail it down to just one thing. However, when I consider my most important attitude in business and life, it's the one on the plaque behind you. Did you see it?"

"Yes." Jack turned to look at the plaque. "When I read that message, Quit Drifting, I knew I needed to ask you what that meant."

"I'm glad you noticed," Brad said. "I have found that most people fall into two distinct categories – they're either doers or drifters. The doers have purpose and are on a mission to fulfill their personal and professional goals in life. The drifters allow external circumstances to determine their next move.

"Those words, Quit Drifting, remind me to stay focused on my most important priorities and to frequently check where I am in relationship to my purpose."

That makes sense, Jack thought to himself. "If you don't mind me asking, *what is* your purpose?"

Brad seemed pleased that Jack was intrigued. "My personal purpose has evolved through the years. In my early years of marriage, my most important priority involved being a great husband. When my children came along, my purpose evolved to becoming a great parent and role model as well as a great husband." Brad paused and Jack could see the gleam in his eyes. "Now, I have twelve grandchildren added to the top of my priority list."

"Congratulations. That is quite a legacy you have. That is awesome." Jack could sense Brad's pride in his family.

Brad proudly showed Jack a photograph of he and his wife surrounded by six children, six in-laws, and twelve grandchildren.

"I know you didn't come today to hear about my family, even though I love talking about them," said Brad, setting the framed photo on his credenza. "Returning to your question about my purpose, in my professional life my purpose has evolved over the years as well. At my age and stage of career, my current purpose is to continue to learn and improve so that I can inspire, encourage and mentor others to help them accomplish their goals."

Jack was energized by Brad's enthusiasm for life and work. "I'm glad you have chosen that purpose. Without your help and the help of other successful people, I may not have had an opportunity to find and pursue my own purpose."

"Great!" Brad responded. "Finding and pursuing your purpose is important. Your purpose is more than a wish or a goal; it's your purposefulness, a higher purpose only you can define. It's your guide that powers everything. Even though it evolves as you go through your life stages, as it has mine, it has permanence. It does not change based on temporary events that occur during each stage.

"Your purpose defines the image you project, how you approach your job, react to surprises, and deal with things that seem unfair. People who understand how their job fits into a broader purpose are more engaged and creative. I believe that my consistency of purpose and my concentration on not allowing myself to drift has been my guiding principle to success."

Brad stopped, smiled and looked intently at Jack. "I've seen many people who have not identified a purpose that they would put above everything. Then, when the next hot deal comes along, they overreact. If you're continuing to create your next new purpose, you really don't have a compass that shows the true direction of where you are heading. You may believe you're winning, but you're not winning at all.

"Without a clear purpose you will drift. You'll move wherever the winds of the moment take you. That's not a good or productive way to exist. No one I've ever known planned to become mediocre in their job or life. But most people who don't have a clear purpose unintentionally allow mediocrity to seep in and they drift along. A friend of mine recently had an experience on holiday that illustrates what I'm talking about:

"He and his wife were vacationing in Maui. Neither of them was a beach veteran but they decided to try snorkeling. Before going out into the ocean on their own, they took snorkeling lessons. Soon they were prepared for their adventure. They got their fins on and masks ready and headed toward the Pacific to discover the unseen beauty of the ocean's depths.

"They were having a great time. No one else was snorkeling in the area. In fact, there was no one within sight. The water was perfect – calm, gentle, and relaxing. As they snorkeled, face-down in the water, the radiantly colored fish, spectacular plant life, and the coral reef fascinated them. It was a remarkable experience, but it was about to become unforgettable.

"My friend lifted his head from the water and looked around. He quickly realized they had drifted out to sea. He could barely see their hotel in the distance. His wife was only a couple of yards from him. When he got her attention, she looked up and immediately recognized the dangerous situation they were in.

"Their relaxing snorkeling adventure was over. They began swimming for their lives toward the shore. They swam for quite a while before finally reaching shallow water where they could stand up and walk to the beach. Once they reached the beach safely, they collapsed in the sand, totally exhausted.

"When they woke up that morning, they had no idea what was in store for them. They had come close to disaster while enjoying what they thought was a peaceful, relaxing time. They had drifted. They did not realize what was happening to them until they looked up. Then they were shocked to find they were not where they began and certainly not where they intended to be."

"Wow, that's frightening. I've heard of people drifting out to sea before," Jack said solemnly. "I'm glad your friends made it back to shore safely."

"Me too," Brad agreed. "Drifting is not unusual in people's personal or professional lives either. Unfortunately, rarely do they drift to a destination they would have chosen. They drift and then ultimately end up trying to 'swim' for their lives. In fact, I think most people drift occasionally. They get caught up in their careers and become distracted and disoriented and lose perspective. Then, they look up to discover they're a long way from where they thought they'd be.

"Life doesn't have to be that way. You have a choice. You can choose to drift or choose to live and work with meaning and purpose. A clearly defined purpose allows you to intervene in any drift that may come your way."

Jack wondered out loud: "So, how do you define and live your purpose? How do you make sure you're not drifting?"

"Those are good questions." Brad's smile dissolved into cool reflection. "Since you spend the majority of your time at work, your purpose has to be in sync with your priorities at home. You have to be critically honest with yourself and answer some challenging questions:

"First, you have to clearly understand who you want to become. I believe that the first principle of success is knowing who you want to become and then having a strong desire to become that person.

"A good question to ask yourself is: How do I want to be described in five years? Ten years? What will people say about me when they deliver my eulogy when that time comes?"

Before Jack had a chance to think about that, Brad suddenly changed course. "Let's take a little break here. Write in your notes your initial thoughts to these questions:"

How do I want to be described in five years:

_____

How do I want to be described in ten years:

_____

How do I want to be remembered by the people who deliver my eulogy:

_____

After allowing a few minutes for Jack to reflect and make notes, Brad continued. "Obviously, you'll need to take time to put more thought into this exercise, but you're off to a good start. Most of the time, your initial reactions will be the foundation for you to create a more detailed plan. Once you understand who you want to become, your purpose will start to become crystal clear.

"After you've answered, *Who do I want to become,* then, ask yourself: *Am I doing the right things to help myself become that person?* To prevent drifting, you have to know where you are. Look around. Who are you becoming? The people around you are most likely reflecting who you're in the process of becoming. They could be helping, or they could be hindering you from achieving your purpose.

"Consider the influence of those you spend your time with. If you spend time with people who use disrespectful language, your language will become like theirs. If you spend time with people with narrow viewpoints, you'll be persuaded by those views. If you spend time with people who are always making excuses about why their life is unfair, you'll tend to do the same thing. But if those you spend time with are positive, hopeful and energetic, you will probably be the same.

"Take a few minutes to reflect and write the answer to three questions:

1. Based on the traits of the people I'm around every day, *who am I becoming right now?*

   _____

2. *Who am I listening to?* Are they a reflection of the person I want to become? Are they encouraging me to become my very best?

   _____

3. *How do people feel when they're around me?* Do they feel better, the same, or worse?

   _____

After a couple of minutes, Brad continued. "Is there a gap between who you want to become and who you are becoming?"

Jack wasn't pleased with his answer. In fact, he was embarrassed by some of his responses. "Yes. Even with just a short time to reflect, it's obvious that there is a significant gap. I'm not very happy with where I am. I can see that I have drifted without even knowing it."

Brad was not surprised. "We all have gaps between what we want and the direction we're heading. The good news is that it's never too late to make adjustments. And most people will move over and allow anyone who knows where they are going to pass by. Now is the time for you to begin passing and closing your gap.

"Your success requires laser-sharp focus. When you answer, 'Who do I want to become and who am I becoming right now?' you have pointed your laser directly at your most important priority.

"The next question to answer is: 'Is your work helping you achieve your purpose?' Your work should be fulfilling, not a burden. Work is a gift and a privilege. If you come to work because it ultimately helps you accomplish your purpose, you'll enjoy your work more and be more productive.

"I have seen intelligent, talented people become miserable because their purpose was out of alignment with their job, which is where they spend most of their time. They fall into a comfortable niche and drift there instead of pursuing their purpose. They allow their careers to stall out to a predictable, boring, unfulfilling day-after-day at work. Every day becomes like that movie, *Groundhog Day*, where you get in a cycle of doing the same things over and over."

"I think I get it," Jack interjected. "I have been living too many 'groundhog days.' I've been going to work because it's required, not because it's helping me fulfill my purpose. Maybe I'm out of sync and my unhappiness at work has created unrelated unhappiness at home. Right now, I'm not doing well in either place."

"Your situation is not uncommon." Brad's demeanor and words were empathic, yet serious. "As I said before, your time at work should be an opportunity to help you become the person you want to be. When you intersect your personal purpose with your job requirements, everything at work will be easier and more fulfilling. If there is a disconnect between the two, you'll be unhappy, unproductive and a negative influence on those around you.

"If what you do at work does not add to your personal purpose in some way – like providing you with the funds, knowledge, skills, time or connections with others who can help guide you toward your purpose – then you may need to make adjustments."

Brad's expression was serious. "This is important. It may not be necessary for you to change jobs for you to fulfill your purpose. In fact, it may be best to not add additional stress by going somewhere new. For example, one person who worked with me was happy in her job. However, she had a deep desire to spend more time with her young children. Recognizing that her children were her true purpose at that stage of her life, she changed roles at work so that she would have the flexibility to spend more time with her kids. Her new flexible hours allowed her work to contribute to her personal purpose at that point in her life. She sacrificed a fancier title and a few extra dollars to be able to work toward her purpose.

"Another person I know had a personal purpose to help the less fortunate in our community. His job provided him the resources, skills and knowledge to help hundreds of people every year. It also provided him connections. Several of his co-workers and their friends invested their time and energy to help him fulfill his purpose. His job did not directly relate to helping the less fortunate, but it provided him the means to become the person he wants to be. The more successful he is at his job, the more funds, knowledge, skills, time and connections he has to live out his purpose."

Brad continued. "Long-term success requires that you live within consistent operating rules that do not change based on the situation of the day. If there's one thing everyone should be able to depend upon, it's the consistency of the rules that govern you. If you know without a doubt what your purpose is, that knowledge alone will take away many of the temptations that result in mistakes."

Jack looked confused. "I'm going to have to put some serious thought into this. My purpose has not been at the top of my mind. That may be why I've drifted to where I am right now. Should I share my purpose with others or just keep it to myself?"

Brad smiled and then warned, "I'm glad you're proactively thinking through what you will do. You don't have to share your purpose with anyone. However, it works best when you have someone, and usually several people, who will hold you accountable. That requires they know what to hold you accountable for. Be aware, you may get some crazy looks of disbelief. Some people will not understand that your purpose drives your life instead of job titles, money, cars, or other material things that drive most people. No, you are more concerned about your life, not your status. That is difficult for some people to understand.

"Another warning is that a clearly defined purpose will not suddenly make your life and career easy. You're still going to have the same challenges you have today. However, your outlook and response to those challenges should be different. Without a clear purpose, your tendency has probably been to overreact to an unexpected, unwanted event. You may have exaggerated both the good things and the bad things going on in your life. When you have a clear purpose, your life will become calmer."

Brad reflected on his experience. "I learned this lesson the hard way. Early in my career, I was doing okay but I thought I could do better. The organization I was working for was going through a tough time. I got impatient. I began interviewing for a better role. I enjoyed having my ego stroked during the job interviews and began believing that I was better than my current job. Ultimately, I left a job that was providing me a solid foundation to build my career to join an organization that offered me nothing but a little more money. It did not take long for me to find out that I'd made a mistake. The tough time at my former organization was temporary. If I'd established a clear purpose, I would not have left. I overreacted, and that mistake set my career back several years.

"So, stay cool and calm. Don't panic. In reality, the bad is not as bad as it seems, but neither is the good as good as you think. Understanding your true purpose helps you maintain more controlled responses to whatever is happening in your life."

"You just described me," Jack said suddenly, jumping into the conversation. "I have been known to overreact to both the good and the bad as it happened to me. In my defense, I have to say it doesn't seem like I'm overreacting at the time it's happening, but looking back, I can see where I may have gotten a little carried away."

Brad then asked: "Have you ever heard the phrase, 'This too shall pass'?'"

"Of course," Jack said. "It's kind of like, nothing lasts forever."

"Actually, I'm not sure where the saying originated," Brad replied, "but Abraham Lincoln shared the following story in 1859:

> It is said an Eastern monarch once charged his wise men to invent for him a sentence, to be ever in view, and which should be true and appropriate in all times and situations.
>
> They presented him the words: 'And this, too, shall pass away.'

"Those words give us hope that, no matter what we are going through, it is temporary."

Brad suddenly stopped talking and seemed deep in thought. Then he continued. "I can attribute much of my success to my unquestionable purpose and the knowledge that 'this too shall pass.' Life is a series of emotions with great heights and great depths. The greatest highs don't last forever, and the deepest lows are not permanent. Stay composed. Be still and remain calm. Whatever is going on in your life, this too shall pass."

"This too shall pass," Jack repeated, even though he was not convinced that was true for him. "But I'm not sure if I will be able to pass with it. This is definitely an area that needs my attention. Is there any other advice you can give me?"

"Since you asked," Brad smiled, leaning back in his chair. "I do have a couple of bonus suggestions. First, be especially careful with your major financial decisions. I have witnessed bad money decisions destroy many people. Take your time and evaluate the ramifications of your decision before pulling the trigger. Be smart with your money. It's difficult to be successful at work or at home when you are continually burdened by bad financial decisions. Do not allow debt to control your life.

"Second, you will become discouraged again somewhere along the way. You'll probably have the tendency to react to something before you get all the facts. Stay cool and don't panic. Bad things happen to even the best people. Even when a situation appears to be the worst, life is still good. Stay positive. It will help make your life better."

Brad continued. "My last thought for you is this: Get on with it. You probably think that you have plenty of time to begin pursuing your purpose, and you may. However, everyone is just one blood test, stress test, X-ray, or serious accident away from a life-changing moment. There's no good reason to put off becoming the person you want to be.

"Nothing would please me more than to watch you become a great role model for others to follow. People are longing to follow someone who is balanced in all areas of life. That person could be you."

"You've given me a lot to think about," Jack said. He thought for a moment and then summed up the session. "But I get what you're saying. Don't drift. Define my purpose. Don't overreact. Control my debt. Get on with it. All of those are challenges to me. This is the straight talk I needed."

"You're on an interesting journey," Brad replied. "My 'Quit Drifting' philosophy is not the beginning or end of achieving success. There are many moving parts that have to work together.

"You may want to visit with a former business associate of mine named Alex Trevino." Brad reached for a business card, wrote her contact information on the back of the card and handed it to Jack. "Here's how you can reach her. She achieved success after experiencing financial and emotional failure. I believe you'll find it interesting when you hear what she has to say. Tell her that I sent you her way."

Jack thanked Brad. As he left the office building, his mind was racing. There was a lot of new information for him to consider.

Brad's Lessons:

I have to precisely understand who I want to become and who I am now in the process of becoming.

Drifting will not lead me where I want to go.

I need to calm down. The good is not as good as it seems; the bad is not as bad as it seems.

I have to get control of my finances. If I'm burdened with a persistent monthly financial crisis, I can't become the person I want to be.

I have to pay attention to those I'm hanging around. I likely will become like them, so is that helping or hurting me?

Whatever challenge I am going through is temporary. This too shall pass.

4
Salute the Truth

Jack was fired up about what he had learned so far on his journey. He was pleasantly surprised that people were willing to share their experience, knowledge, passion and wisdom. Their 'secrets' were not really secrets. The people he had talked to wanted to help him become just as prosperous as they were. Their knowledge was an open book for anyone who asked.

Jack certainly knew Alex Trevino by name. In their town she was legendary for her accomplishments, but he'd also heard that her route to prosperity hadn't been smooth. Jack had heard stories about how Alex had risen from being dead broke to become the ultra-successful person she was today. Jack had wanted to meet her for years but never had the opportunity. Brad had opened the door, and this was his chance to finally meet her.

Arriving at her office's reception area a few minutes early for their meeting, Jack noticed several framed national magazine covers adorning the walls. Each cover prominently featured Alex's picture. The headlines read, "Turnaround of the Year," "Rising from the Ashes" and "Entrepreneur of the Year." He silently nodded in admiration. Alex's accomplishments were even more impressive than he'd heard. But he couldn't help but wonder about the back story.

At exactly the scheduled appointment time, Alex appeared. The room lit up with her energy when she entered. Her contagious smile, attractiveness and impeccable dress made a splendid first impression. They made their way to the conference room where Alex asked Jack about himself, his family, his journey and what he had discovered thus far. He filled her in on his experiences and expressed how grateful he was to meet with her. She was gracious with his compliments and then asked how she could help.

Jack briefly told her about each person he'd interviewed and the most important principle that had helped each of them become successful. "However, they each said that their achievements required more than just doing one thing well. The one question I've asked every person is this: Is there one particular principle you believe has most influenced your success? I'm interested in your answer as well."

"Thank you for asking. I'm glad that Brad recommended you call me." Alex paused before continuing. "I don't know if you are aware, but my success did not come easy. It was preceded by a devastating failure. It was a lonely, scary time for me."

"Yes, I'm familiar with at least some of it," Jack said. "Your story is legendary. I had not seen the impressive magazine covers until today, but I've been told you've been a positive inspiration to people all over the country."

"Thanks for your kind words," Alex smiled. "It seems people enjoy reading or hearing comeback stories. Unfortunately, there is no comeback without a setback. I think most successful people are the result of persisting beyond failures – and usually not just one, but many that enable them to determine their unique route to success. I learned that lesson the hard way, and believe it or not, my failures became my pathway to success.

"Not that long ago, I was broke. I didn't have enough money to pay attention – much less pay my bills. I had made several major mistakes. I hired the wrong people, rushed into decisions, didn't listen to my employees, discounted my customers' feedback, made bad financial decisions and many other blunders. Before I hit bottom, I thought I was invincible. Failure, I was convinced, was not something that would happen to me.

"Well, I found out that I'm not invincible. Like everyone else, I'm vulnerable to failure and when it happened to me, it hit me hard. At that point I reached rock bottom, my lowest of lows. While I was deep in my own introspection, I discovered that I had ignored the harsh truth of my situation. That is when I latched onto my most significant principle: *Salute the Truth.*

Jack recognized Alex's humility. "Thank you for your candor," he said. "I didn't know the extent of your challenges. What do you mean when you say, 'salute the truth'?"

"There were challenges, for sure," Alex acknowledged.

"However, I learned some of my most valuable lessons through those mistakes and failures. Based on my experiences, success is a lousy teacher. Walt Disney once said, 'You might not realize it when it happens, but a kick in the teeth may be the best thing in the world for you.' Now that I've experienced a kick in the teeth and learned from it, I can agree with him.

"Failing was not fun, but since then I've observed that most successful people fail faster and more often than the average person. I learned enough from failure to finally achieve some success. Thanks to those experiences, I realize it's okay to fail – everyone fails at one time or another – but it's not okay to keep failing at the same thing. And it's not okay to not learn from your failures."

Alex reflected on Jack's question. "You asked me what it means to 'salute the truth.' I use the word salute because saluting is a sign of respect and acknowledgement. In the past I would have said that I needed to welcome or embrace the truth. But I didn't want to. However, I had to respect the truth, acknowledge it and move forward regardless of how I felt about it. One of the main reasons I failed is that I turned my back to the truth. And it's probably the same for others who fail. Not only do they not salute the truth, but they also continue to believe something is true when it isn't."

Alex paused and reflected. "One of the toughest things to figure out is, 'What's the truth?' That sounds pretty crazy, doesn't it? Why do you think that figuring out the truth is so difficult?"

Jack thought for a moment. "Well, maybe they don't have all the information they need to recognize the truth. Or, maybe the truth changes, or it takes a long time to figure out and they arrive at their conclusion too quickly."

Alex acknowledged that each of Jack's answers had merit in specific situations. "In addition, though, some people want the truth to be different, so they shun reality. They ignore the truth, just like I did.

"It seems to me that we tend to make up things that align with our hopes and dreams. And the truth is sometimes camouflaged by politics, personal agendas, pride, or feelings that blind us. Without realizing it, we deceive ourselves and believe what we desperately want to believe. Trust me, it's never a good idea to lie to yourself, no matter how painful the truth may be. You have to respect the truth."

Jack was listening intently. What she'd said had hit close to home. Although he was uncomfortable admitting his mistakes, he decided to share his experience. "I can relate to everything you just said. Now that you mention it, I guess I did turn my back on the reality of my situation. There certainly wasn't any saluting going on, probably because I didn't want to admit to myself, or anyone else, that things had become as stagnant as they were. My pride would not allow me to accept the real truth. It's embarrassing. I hate that I put myself in that position."

"You're not alone," Alex said in reassuring voice. "In my case, I was completely convinced my decisions were best for everyone – even after a decision led to failure. I confirmed my decisions with people who were similar to me – same background, values and opinions. I asked their opinions after I had passionately expressed my own opinion to them. Actually, I was making decisions based on one opinion – mine. Looking back, it's obvious why I made so many mistakes; I was not dealing with the truth.

"After coming to that realization, I decided that the real truth needed to be the catalyst for every decision in my life. I had to learn to quit making things up to look the way I wanted them to be. I was too comfortable kicking reality under the carpet and trying to ignore it. That didn't do me any good."

Jack nodded, but inside he was squirming. His own story was eerily similar to Alex's. "I think we all do that when we don't want to believe something. I know I do my share of kicking."

Alex smiled, nodded in agreement, and continued. "I had to learn how to search for the truth. It was up to me to rebel against my natural tendencies to believe what I wanted to believe, and instead salute the real truth faster. I had to train myself to examine the facts and separate them from my feelings and my ego. When I didn't understand the real truth, I corrected the wrong things. Once I understood what my reality was, I could make corrections and improvements. Then, my road to success became a little straighter, the challenges seemed less overwhelming, my goals were within easier reach, and I had fewer surprises along the way.

"Looking back, I learned from my failures, but I refused to keep learning the same thing over and over. I promised myself I would never make the same mistake again. I began hiring tougher, requested more information before making important decisions and began listening carefully to my team and our customers. My decisions became better. Then, the next time I made a mistake, I moved on and didn't make that same mistake again.

Alex paused for a moment. "In an effort to provide you with the whole truth of my journey, I must admit that some of my failures scarred me deeply. So deep, in fact, that I became afraid to take any risks at all. My fear of failure became a powerful force against me, and I would try anything to avoid putting myself in a position where I might fail. I eventually came to realize that most of the really good stuff in life requires taking a risk. I could not allow my fear of failure to prevent me from trying.

"I hated failing. However, the scars from my failures eventually healed and became beauty marks. When I look back, I see failure taught me humility, perseverance and courage. I learned that my failures were important lessons that helped lead me toward my success. They also taught me to do whatever was necessary to prevent putting myself in the same situation again."

Jack interrupted Alex. "That's a pretty incredible realization. Your scars from your failures healed and became your beauty marks. I need to remember that."

"Yes, it *was* an incredible realization," Alex emphasized. "Also, to my amazement, my greatest accomplishments arrived shortly after my most devastating defeats. After my disappointments, I had to press on and continue. To my surprise, after I was convinced that I was surrounded by insurmountable adversity, my most defining moments appeared. After that discovery, I began searching for a great success after every devastating disappointment … and you'd be surprised how often it happened.

"Your journey will have bumps along the way. Don't allow them to derail you – acknowledge the missteps, learn from them and continue pursuing your dream. Just don't duplicate your mistakes."

Jack smiled half-heartedly. "I must admit, I'm surprised at your story. I made the assumption that you hadn't made the same or as many mistakes as others. But you've taught me that you had the wisdom to learn from your mistakes and make adjustments to prevent those mistakes from happening again."

"Exactly," Alex responded. "Success rarely appears on the first try. It appears after trial, error, continued effort and moving forward after failure. If you asked some of my friends nearing the end of their careers about their regrets, they would rarely admit to regretting things they did. Most would say they regretted *not* doing something because they had feared they might fail."

Alex paused before continuing. "Another mistake was thinking that I knew the truth before I heard the entirety of what people were saying. I was a terrible listener. I would react before the person told me everything. Subconsciously, I suppose I considered myself a psychic who could accurately read other people's thoughts like: *'This is what he really means … He thinks I don't know what he is talking about … He is going to say no … or He doesn't like me.'*"

Alex laughed at this absurdity. "Eventually, I came to accept the reality that I was not a mind reader and I couldn't know what another person was thinking until I asked them. It's a bad assumption to believe you know what anyone else is thinking.

"To salute the truth, you have to focus, pay close attention to what is being said, ask questions, actively listen, and acknowledge the real truth quickly."

Jack hesitated before he spoke. "I think everyone could probably listen better. I know I could. As you were talking, I thought you were talking about my mind-reading expertise."

"I wasn't thinking of just you, or anyone else," Alex affirmed. "I was talking about me, too. I have to keep reminding myself that the biggest room in my house is the room for improvement. There's always something I can do better, more often or with a different intensity. Becoming a better listener is still at the top of my list.

"Ironically, some of the best advice I ever received on how to improve has come from criticism," Alex went on. "I hate to be criticized, but criticism has helped me focus my attention on what I need to do to make better decisions."

Jack nodded in agreement and then confessed, "All my life, I've heard people boast, 'I welcome constructive criticism,' but I find that hard to believe. I really don't like to be criticized either."

"I get it," Alex nodded. "Criticism carries a certain sting, even though it may help us correct a wrong, strengthen a weakness or chart a better course. One reason that criticism stings is our inclination to think our idea is the best – or the only – idea that will work. If you believe that and you're closed to any suggestions, you then become stagnated in your own stubbornness."

"So, how do you handle criticism?" Jack said, eager to learn. "I need some pointers because I either bow up and get defensive, or I shut down when someone begins criticizing me."

Alex was pleased that Jack was asking good questions. "I was, and sometimes I still am, defensive about criticism that comes my way. However, I've found that using criticism as a learning tool literally changed me. Here are a few suggestions that helped me come to that realization:

1. Acknowledge that **criticism is a form of feedback – and** you need feedback to improve in any area of your life. Whether the criticism is constructive or destructive, allow yourself some time to think before responding. Your emotions react faster than your thoughts, so allow your thoughts time to catch up before reacting.

2. Ask yourself these questions: **Who's offering the criticism?** Are they qualified? Are they trying to hurt or trying to help? Objectively, is there any truth to what he or she is saying?

   If the person is qualified to comment, trying to help, and there is at least a kernel of truth in what they're saying, pay close attention. They are handing you a gift … make sure you accept it that way.

   If the criticism is from someone who has an alternative agenda, or who is not qualified to offer constructive criticism anyway, thank them and let it go.

3. **Repeat back the criticism** as you understand it. Sometimes we get into trouble responding to what we thought we heard, and not what was actually said. Repeating the criticism confirms your understanding and ensures that you respond correctly.

4. Listen to what's being said but **try not to take it personally.** Don't allow your self-esteem to be at the mercy of others. The critic is not attacking you – they are criticizing your attitudes or actions.

Jack was bothered by something Alex had said, and he needed to clear it up. "You said that criticism should be received as a gift. That kind of gift is difficult for me to accept."

Alex smiled as though she felt the same way. "I agree. Most people don't view criticism as a gift. However, criticism can be a necessary part of growth, even if it's from someone you may not like. You need constructive criticism, no matter how successful you become. Criticism whips your fragmented attention into a concentrated focus on a change you may need to make.

"Criticism from the right people will lead to improvements you would probably never have made, because you didn't know you needed to change.

"The healthy approach to criticism is to pay attention to it," Alex emphasized. "Listen with the intent to understand why the criticism is being leveled at you, and why the critic may want you to consider a different perspective. And sometimes, it's good to not take yourself so seriously. You don't think you do everything perfectly all the time, do you? Of course not. Try to allow yourself some levity in accepting criticism."

Alex paused and added, "While we're discussing criticism, I think we need to touch on another area – when someone is a constant critic of almost everything you do. That person may be relentless and ruthless with their criticism, even if it's justified."

Alex suddenly interrupted herself. "That relentless personal critic reminds me of a story ... follow me on this:

"Once there was a farmer who advertised his 'frog farm' for sale. The farm, he claimed, had a pond filled to the brim with fine bullfrogs.

"When a prospective buyer appeared, the farmer asked him to return that evening so he might hear the frogs in full voice. When the buyer returned, he was favorably impressed by the symphony of magical melodies emanating from the pond. He bought the farm on the spot.

"A few weeks later, the new owner decided to drain the pond so that he could catch and market the plentiful supply of frogs. To his amazement, when the water was drained from the pond, he found that one old, loudmouth bullfrog had made all the noise."

Alex explained: "That story may reflect the people who relentlessly criticize you. Don't allow the critical noise of one, or even a few, old 'bullfrogs' to keep you from doing what you need to do."

"I like that story," Jack shot back, smiling. "I tend to dwell on the noise from that one old 'bullfrog' and it wears me out. Maybe it's time for me to gig that frog and move on. I'm my own worst critic. Actually, most of the time I'm the loudmouth bullfrog in the pond who is relentless in my self-criticism. Your story applies to me."

Alex beamed, obviously happy with Jack's connection to the bullfrog story. Then she leaned forward and asked in a serious tone. "Aren't we all most critical of ourselves? Learning to forgive myself was not easy, either.

"We talked earlier about some of my greatest failures. When you experience a significant failure, you take it personally. One of my most difficult, but most important, lessons was to learn to forgive myself for my own blunders. I had to find peace within myself. You may think that would be easy, but it wasn't. In fact, it was very hard for me because I would dwell on my mistakes. My past was my place of residence. That is *not* a good place to live. Until I made peace with myself, I could never fully enjoy living. It took me some time to realize it was counterproductive to beat myself up and not let it go. And, if I'm honest with myself, the statute of limitations had expired on most of the things I couldn't forgive myself for. I had to convince myself that I was okay. I was human and had gotten off course. I had just made a mistake. Then, I had to allow myself the freedom to continue.

"Along those same lines, I had to learn to forgive, and to ask for forgiveness, from some other people as well. Harboring resentment made me miserable. Some of my friends abandoned me when I needed them most. Looking back, I'm still puzzled about why they did what they did. Regardless, it was up to me to forgive them and ask for their forgiveness, so I'd be free to move forward. I had to learn that chasing after a poisonous snake that had bitten me did not solve any of my problems. It was better for me to move in another direction and allow those who had distanced themselves from me to go their own way as well."

Jack interrupted. "Wait. Why would *you* need to ask for forgiveness? Aren't they the ones who abandoned you? I think it would be tough enough to forgive them, much less ask them to forgive you. It doesn't make sense."

"I appreciate what you're saying," Jack's new mentor pointed out. "But you and I are looking at the situation solely from my perspective. I didn't know if I had done something to contribute to the issue. Asking them to forgive me was humbling, but once I'd asked, then I was free to let go without worrying further. Asking forgiveness marked an ending for all of us, and it was the best thing for me to do. There is no rule that states that the person who committed the offense has to ask for or deserves forgiveness. I had to learn that forgiveness would probably mean more to me than to the person I'm forgiving ... and that was okay. For me, not forgiving was more destructive.

"Also, my forgiveness had to be without attachments. If I forgave someone while expecting something in return, I was not forgiving at all; I was trading. Forgiving has to be a gift, not a trade exchanged with someone with an expectation of something in return. You should never include the phase 'If I have offended you' or 'If I was wrong.' Eliminate the 'If I' and ask for their forgiveness without attachments.

"I discovered that forgiving others was actually a gift to myself. If the other person accepted my forgiveness, that was a bonus. Whether or not they accepted my forgiveness, I could not continue to allow my past to eat my future."

"Your past was eating your future?" Jack furiously wrote this phrase in his notes. "I can relate to that."

Alex allowed a few seconds before continuing. "Yes. Don't allow yourself to forsake your future because of your past. You have the exclusive power over your future. There is no reason for you to accept and settle for status quo or surrender as a victim of circumstances. Take authority over your life."

Alex looked at her watch. "I have to get to my next meeting in a few minutes, but I'll leave one last thought with you: Two common attributes I have observed among successful people are that **they do not make excuses** to justify why things are the way they are, and **they don't complain** about the way things should be. They take charge to make better things happen. They clean up the rubble from their past mistakes so that they can begin to rebuild. That is what you are doing on your journey. You're going to be fine."

Alex began wrapping up the session. "I enjoyed sharing my experiences. I hope this time was beneficial for you. Remember: Salute the truth. Regardless of how you may be tempted to manipulate it, the truth is the truth."

Jack was not ready to leave, but he was grateful to Alex for making time for him. "You are a remarkable person," Jack said, rising to shake Alex's hand. "Our time together has been too short, but I'm grateful you shared your backstory with me. I had no idea you overcame many of the same challenges I am facing."

Alex continued to mentor as she escorted Jack toward the door. "As I'm sure many people you've visited have told you, success is not found in just one principle. It's a combination of many truths. I suggest you talk to Herb Hill. He has done some great things in our community. I don't personally know him, but I think it would be valuable to hear his perspective on his own journey toward success."

Jack thanked Alex and left her office feeling hopeful. The advice she'd given was both important and practical. He'd been a champion at seeing what he wanted to see and believing what he wanted to believe. It was time for him to begin saluting the truth.

Alex's Lessons:

There is no need to learn the same thing over and over. Once is enough.

Failure is my teacher. Pay attention. My scars from failure can become beauty marks.

I will no longer be a relentless personal critic of myself.

I am not a mind reader. I need to become a great listener.

I search for a great success after a devastating disappointment. I will not allow my past to eat my future.

I ask for forgiveness when there is any question about my role in a situation that has become harmful.

I forgive myself, and others, without expecting anything in return.

Consider it Done

Jack's journey had sent him in several unexpected directions. He was pleasantly surprised at how willingly his accomplished advisors recommended he talk to their peers. They were secure in their beliefs and enjoyed sharing how they had reached a measure of success. There was plenty of knowledge and wisdom for everyone, and they were pleased to share their experiences.

His next stop was a visit with Herb Hill. Herb traveled extensively as a human resource executive for a chain of hotels, and it was a challenge to get on his calendar. The only time available to meet was over lunch so they agreed to meet at a restaurant near Herb's office.

Jack arrived early and secured a table. Soon after, Herb arrived. Jack recognized him from his picture in the business section of the newspaper and motioned him over to his table.

They formally met for the first time. Herb was an average height, middle-aged, greying guy whose beaming smile exuded confidence and happiness.

After several minutes of exchanging stories about mutual friends, Jack shared that Alex Trevino had suggested they talk. Herb was surprised. "Alex recommended me? I have never met her, but I know her by reputation. I'm flattered she thinks enough of me to send you in my direction."

"Not only did she send me in your direction, but she was sure you would have a unique perspective on achieving success," Jack said. I'm eager to learn from your experiences." After a few minutes of talking casually and placing their lunch order, Jack asked his most important question: "Is there one particular principle you think has contributed the most to your success?"

Without hesitation, Herb confidently answered. "For sure! That's an easy question for me. Many years ago, I noticed most people won't do what they say. They might do part of it, but rarely all. It probably wasn't intentional, but they just didn't follow through completely. That discovery led me to become aware of how often people fail to do what they say. My findings were alarming. I was surprised that people often say a lot yet do a little.

"At about that same time, I hired an administrative assistant, a wonderful person whose attitude was positive, energetic and upbeat. When I asked her to complete her first assignment, she immediately responded: '*Consider it done.*' I asked her what she meant, and she explained I could mark that project down as done. I thought 'Wow. That is a great attitude.' But I was skeptical. I thought it was probably nothing more than nice words … words she thought I wanted to hear.

"Much to my surprise and delight, well before the project was due, she delivered it to me. Her work was even better than what I'd expected. Her three simple words – *Consider it done* – were real. I didn't realize it at the time, but it was her operating philosophy. *Consider it done* reflected her dependability and confidence. She immediately made great strides toward earning my trust.

"After that day, I began thinking about her words '*Consider it done.*' Most people around me at that time would say, 'I'll try.' There's a big difference between 'I'll try' and '*Consider it done.*' 'I'll try' is often used as an excuse for *not* doing. You're not committed to actually doing something when you use those words. The message 'I'll try' sends is weak and apathetic.

"*Consider it done* is more than just words strung together. It is an integrity statement. When you say, *Consider it done* the message is direct and powerful. From the day I first heard my assistant say *Consider it done* I began eliminating the words 'I'll try' from my conversations and I asked those around me to do the same.

"From that day forward, every person on our team began doing *all* that needed to be done – no more jobs were done halfway. Occasionally we had to renegotiate the project up front, but then we would walk away and *Consider it done* with confidence. I began noticing the positive impact of being able, without hesitation, to depend upon the word of everyone in our organization. It eliminated stress, doubt and frustrations when people did exactly what they said they'd do."

Herb's voice was stern as he continued, "Then, we began measuring what we called our say/do ratio. It was a simple formula – how often did you say something vs. how often did you do it. The say/do ratio is a close relative to *Consider it done.* It's one way to measure your integrity. It's important because doing or not doing what you say is the quickest way to earn or lose trust. When you commit to something, write it down and make sure that, at a bare minimum, you do exactly what you say. You don't want a say/do ratio that reflects that you say more than you do. Before committing to something, stop and ask yourself: 'Do I really intend to act on this'? If you can't confidently say, *Consider it done* then don't commit to it."

Jack interjected. "Wait. If I understand correctly, you really want a say/do ratio of better than 1:1, right? You wouldn't do just what you say, but more."

"That would be great!" Herb encouraged. "You're thinking right. I heard someone express it like this: 'Do what you say you're going to do. And do it a little better than you said you would.' That is a good goal for all of us.

"Your integrity is your most precious personal possession, but you have to guard and protect it. If people can't depend on you to *Consider it done* your integrity is at risk.

"Early in my career, I learned that if I was consistent with my word and did my very best to do the right thing, everything else would take care of itself. Eventually you'll know what the right thing to do is and you'll always know if what you say is true. I also learned that people forgive and forget judgment errors, but rarely does anyone forget integrity mistakes."

"I feel like my integrity has remained pretty solid even during my tough times," Jack responded somewhat defensively.

"That's great," Herb nodded. "However, you may be judging your integrity on a different scale than the people you interact with do. A lot of people discount simple, common, and seemingly harmless statements like 'I'll call you later,' or 'I'll keep you informed' or 'I'll get right on it.' You may believe those statements don't count, but they do. When it comes to the perspective of others, *everything* counts."

"If I'm counting those minor commitments, maybe I have slipped a little," Jack admitted. "My intention is to always *Consider it done* when I say it, but I have to admit, I will occasionally commit to some things, especially minor things, that I never get around to doing."

Herb nodded in agreement. "Most people say things they don't follow through on at some time or another. Unfortunately, no one can judge whether you intended to follow through or not. They can only evaluate what you do. You may want people to allow you the grace of not counting minor commitments. But people will judge you on what they think about you, not what *you believe* they should think about you. My point is that everything counts when it comes to your word. Even the small, minor commitments count."

Jack wasn't thrilled about what he was hearing. After thinking for a minute, he shared, "I've probably discounted how my integrity was being evaluated when I made what I thought was an insignificant commitment. I guess I need to be more aware that everything counts, like you said."

"If someone fails to keep a small, insignificant commitment, why do you think they would keep a large, significant one?" Herb asked rhetorically. "I don't think most people intentionally lie, but I've seen expense reports padded, resumes exaggerated, ineligible tax deductions claimed, and have witnessed people take credit for someone else's work. All of those are integrity breaches."

Jack added, "Yes, I've seen those same things, but I rationalized it as one of those little white lies everyone tells occasionally."

Herb countered, "Maybe everyone tells a little white lie occasionally. However, you have to ask yourself, 'when is a lie small enough not to matter?' Is there a line you cross where that little lie becomes big enough to suddenly matter? If so, who determines where that line is? I don't think there is such a line. There is no lie that doesn't matter. Truth is absolute, not relative. You need to be honest with 100% precision as best you can.

"When you think about it, it's obvious how important an attitude of *Consider it done* is to those around you. Everyone wants to know, without a doubt, that you will do what you say. I believe your integrity has the single greatest impact on your long-term success. It is the 'oil' that keeps relationships running smooth. It is the cornerstone of trust."

Herb continued. "Also, the loss of integrity is a major reason for failure. Look at the people who make the news every evening because of some scandal – sports figures, film stars, politicians, CEOs or a neighbor down the street. What most of them share is that, somewhere along the way, they sacrificed their integrity.

"My assistant nailed it – without integrity and trust, nothing else really matters. It doesn't matter what you say if no one trusts you. And, it doesn't matter how committed, skilled, courageous or optimistic you are if people don't believe you'll honor what you say. None of those traits matter if people can't positively *Consider it done.*

"I became keenly aware and protective of my commitments," Herb continued. "From that point forward, I would not commit to something without first having the time, resources, and true intention to make it happen. That was a turning point in my career. Also, you may be interested in knowing that the administrative aide who taught me to *Consider it done* has been promoted several times. It was the turning point for her career as well."

"So, her three simple words had that great of an impact on your success?" Jack asked.

"Absolutely!" Herb responded instantly. "There are more than words within that phrase. There is confidence, commitment and accountability. It reflects an attitude of moving forward. *Consider it done* – who wouldn't want to hear those words? Think about it. What if everyone on your team was of the same mind? What if everyone could *Consider it done* when a commitment was made? It would literally change your career and your life."

"If my integrity is so important, what can I do to protect it?" Jack was eager to know.

"That's a good question!" Herb was prepared to share his experience. "I believe if you consciously do three things, you will enhance your relationships, improve trust and become a person whom others want to be around more often.

"First, ask yourself the basic integrity check: ***Is the action I am about to take illegal, immoral or unethical in any form?*** If you answer yes to any of those, STOP. Period. There is never a good reason to do anything that's illegal, immoral or unethical … in any form.

"Second, **defend your commitments.** Don't make any commitments you cannot keep. A lot of people have a tough time saying no. Then they hope no one remembers they said yes to something. That is a trust-destroying habit. You may have to give up something to make your commitment. If that's the case, ask yourself, am I okay with making the exchange?

"Third, **when you commit to something, write it down and do it**. Create a commitment folder so you can check yourself frequently.

"Of course, there are rare occasions when something will prevent you from doing what you said. When that happens, communicate it immediately. Don't wait even a minute. People deserve time to react if you have an emergency that prevents you from doing what you said you would do.

"I know I want to be around people who will live up to their word. Don't you?" Herb asked rhetorically. "Absolutely! That's why *Consider it done* has been so important to me."

The time at lunch had flown by, and Jack realized it was time to go. He completed his notes, then said: "You have given me a lot to consider. Frankly, I didn't realize that my integrity was being judged and monitored by every small commitment that I made. It never occurred to me that my success could be dependent upon my say/do ratio. I will take your words to heart.

"As I mentioned to you," Jack said as they shook hands, "I'd like to continue my journey and visit a few other people who could advise me as you have. Is there someone you recommend I visit?"

"As a matter of fact, there is," Herb said. "One person who has had an incredible, positive influence in my life is Audrey

Kruger. She is one of the most optimistic and helpful people I have ever known. I think you will like her."

"I will reach out to her," Jack promised. "You can consider it done. And thank you for meeting with me. Your advice has been terrific. I look forward to speaking with Audrey and getting her counsel as well. From what you've said, it sounds like she'll be a positive influence for me. Staying positive is an area where I struggle sometimes. Thanks for the recommendation."

Herb's Lessons:

When I make a commitment, you can confidently 'Consider it done.'

I have to protect and guard my integrity. It is my most precious possession.

My say/do ratio is a minimum of 1:1.

There is no lie that is so insignificant that it doesn't matter.

I have to be honest with 100% precision.

6

Lift the Fog

Jack contacted Audrey Kruger and they agreed to meet at her office at 7:00 a.m. Audrey owned a manufacturing company that had been in her family for over fifty years, and Jack knew she was a pillar of the community and he was excited to meet with her.

Jack left his home allowing plenty of time to spare and arrive on time. However, when he approached the bridge that he needed to cross to reach her office, it was temporarily closed to all traffic. The fog over the water was so thick that he couldn't see beyond the hood of his car.

Jack was concerned that he and Audrey would have to postpone the meeting. He called Audrey and she immediately relieved his anxiety when she said, "No problem. Not to worry. I will move some things around. Come after the fog lifts."

By 8 a.m. the fog had lifted. The sky was clear. Almost immediately, everything changed, and Jack could see for miles. It was a strange shift from the dense-thick fog to a crystal-clear sky.

Jack arrived at Audrey's office at 8:15. He checked in with the receptionist and waited a few minutes before Audrey met him in the lobby. She had a glowing smile, self-assured handshake and a positive, energetic, attitude. She confidently owned her space.

Audrey led him to her office and motioned for him to sit in a comfortable chair across from her desk. She then began the dialogue. "Thank you for coming in this morning. I'm sorry the bridge was closed. That rarely happens. But look at the spectacular day it has become. I appreciate you calling me to let me know you would be late. I was able to move some things around; it was not a problem.

"Tell me about your journey," she asked. "I'd be interested in what you have learned. I'm sure that I, too, could use some of the advice you've gathered."

Jack was happy to share the results of his visits thus far. "It's been quite an adventure. The lessons that other people have shared have made me think about areas I hadn't considered before. Without going into too much detail, my career and life had become mundane and stagnant. It led me to ask several successful people, like you, if they would share with me their philosophy about business and life.

"I'm about midway through my visits. So far, I've learned I have to take control and blast my way through my tough times. I have to be open to change and closed to complacency. I have to get a better grip on my purpose so I don't drift into areas where I don't want to go. I also learned that there is never a good reason to lie to myself – I have to salute the truth. And, I have to protect my integrity. That just skims the surface of what I've learned. I'm hoping to add to my list this morning."

"I hope so too," Audrey agreed. "That is quite an education you've been given. Most people don't take the time or effort to address their situation like you're doing. So, tell me, how can I help you this morning?"

"I'm here to learn from you," Jack explained. "I admire what you have accomplished, and I would like to know if there is one particular principle you think has had the most impact on your success."

Audrey smiled and she seemed pleased to respond. "That is a great question. Thank you for asking. Yes, I had a defining moment in my career. It occurred several years ago when I was struggling in my business. The economy was soft, our products were behind schedule and I was losing my best employees. The only thing I could see at the time was a bad economy and delayed production. My personal fog was much denser than the fog you faced this morning.

"That's when a respected acquaintance and advisor told me that regardless of the situation I was facing, '*Something can be done, and there is always something I can do.*' Those words stuck with me and I have leaned on them. That person gave me a wonderful gift."

Jack was curious. "What did you do?"

"I took him at his word. I started evaluating my situation. I wrote down my thoughts about what could be done and what I could do. One thing that jumped out at me was that because of the economy and production issues, I had allowed my most valuable assets – our people – to leave and go to other organizations facing the same economy. And those organizations were facing other issues as well. I'll spare you all the details, but I discovered that the wisdom he shared with me was true. I had to adjust my focus from what was not happening to what could happen, and from why I could not do something to what I could do. It changed my perspective, and it changed my career.

"My advisor was right. There were lots of things that could be done and plenty of things that I could do.

"Those words have been a source of strength since that day. *Something can be done* – the situation is not permanent, so something can be done right now. And *there is always something I can do*; the next move is always mine to take."

"I hear what you are saying." Jack hesitated before continuing his thoughts. "But when I'm stuck in a situation, I have a hard time figuring out what to do. Going forward is tricky because I can't see where I should be going. Do you really believe there is *always* something that can be done? And is the next move *always* mine?"

"Absolutely." Audrey smiled and then explained. "It may not be an action you can readily see. For instance, on your trip here this morning, was there anything you could do about the fog?"

"No. That was what I was thinking. There was nothing I could do to lift the fog. I was stuck." Jack was sure that he made his point.

Audrey asked, "So, what did you do? You called me and explained the situation. How did you feel when you had to call me?"

Jack reflected. "I was a little stressed. I worried you wouldn't be able to change our meeting time and it would have to be postponed or cancelled. I prayed the fog would lift quickly."

"So, correct me if I'm wrong," Audrey instructed, "but it seems to me you took the best course of action available to you. Lifting the fog was not something you could control, but if you'd done nothing, you would have no-showed and our meeting would have been cancelled. You were not responsible for the foggy conditions this morning; you were responsible for the decisions you made because of the fog. You called, prayed and had patience for the fog to lift. Something could be done ... and you did it."

"I can't take credit for the patience part," Jack confided. "That is not one of my strong attributes. I didn't look at calling you as taking ownership of the situation. I assumed the only appropriate action was for the fog to lift."

"I'm glad the fog rolled in this morning." Audrey surprised Jack with her statement, and then she asked him a random question. "How much water do you think it takes to create dense fog like we had this morning?"

"I have no idea," Jack said. "Hundreds, maybe thousands of gallons of water?"

Audrey continued, "I read that fog covering seven city blocks, 100 feet deep – about like our fog this morning – is composed of about one glass of water. Can you believe that small amount of water can create enough density to close a bridge? The fog was not permanent. It was a temporary state created by a very small amount of an ordinary substance.

"It seems to me most people create their own fog. The two great fog generators for many people are constant worry and persistent negative emotions, such as pessimism, fear and doubt. Both worry and negative emotions create fog so thick that you can't see how to move forward.

"Let's think about what we worry about. Earl Nightingale, one of the first personal development gurus, studied the effects of worry. He concluded that 40 percent of the time we worry about things that will never happen. Forty percent! That's a lot of time, emotion and energy spent on things that never happen."

"I've heard that statistic before," Jack said. "It is pretty alarming when you think about it. I also heard that worrying must work since only 40 percent of what we worry about happens." He gave Audrey a wry smile.

Audrey laughed. "That's funny, but worrying doesn't prevent anything from happening – and that look on your face tells me you know that. The same study found that 30 percent of our worries are in the past and cannot be changed, and 12 percent are worries about criticism from others that is mostly untrue. We worry about our health 10 percent of the time, which usually only makes our health worse. Only 8 percent of our worries are real problems we'll have to face – and out of those, only half of them are under our control.

"Worry will paralyze you – and not much good happens when you're paralyzed by worry. It becomes a dense fog, like we had this morning, which prevents you from seeing a path forward."

Audrey then asked Jack, "Have you ever had the wind knocked out of you?"

"Yes," Jack quickly replied. "Many times during my football days. It's the worst feeling ever."

"It is frightening," Audrey agreed. "I had my wind knocked out several times in my soccer career. Each incident probably lasted only a few seconds, but that breathless moment seemed forever. During the time it took to recover, I could not even move.

"Worry is like having your wind knocked out. In fact, the word 'worry' comes from a word meaning "to choke or strangle." It is to torment oneself with, or suffer from, disturbing thoughts. It creates fear, drains your energy and prevents you from being your best."

"I'm guilty of worrying as much as anyone else," Jack acknowledged. "But I think it's human nature to worry. Is there really anything I can do to stop worrying?"

"Remember, something can be done and there is *always* something you can do," Audrey reinforced. "I've put a lot of thought into why I worry and what I should be doing instead of worrying. Write these thoughts down about how to lift the worry fog:

"First, **Stop fortunetelling**. You said you were worried this morning that I would cancel our meeting, yet you had never met me. Why were you worried about that? Did you have any reason to believe that? Did you really think you could predict my reaction? No one is brilliant enough to make a great decision without understanding the facts. Most worry is based on false assumptions – things you fear will happen, and not the facts of what is happening. Stop fortunetelling. Get the facts before worrying about something that will only drain your energy. Be honest and ask yourself, what are the real odds that what I'm worrying about will even happen?

"Next, **Don't try to control the uncontrollable.** Be honest with yourself and determine what you can control. You could not prevent the fog, but you did have control over how you reacted to the fog. Act on what you can control.

"Then, **Analyze – what is the worst possible outcome?** If your worry is among the small number of things you *can* control, what's the worst that can happen? The worst outcome this morning was that our meeting would be cancelled. That would probably not have been as disastrous as you thought. You could live with the eventual outcome, even though you'd have to make some changes.

"**Get busy and do what you can.** If you have any control over the situation, create a plan to ensure that the worst does not happen. It's difficult to worry about things you're diligently trying to improve.

"Finally, **As best you can, let it go.** If you've done everything you can, let it go. Your worrying is not helping anyone or anything. In fact, it may be making you and those around you miserable."

"It's difficult for me to go through that process," Jack admitted, genuinely wanting to understand more. "This morning's situation in the fog was different. It wasn't that complicated to call your office and let you know my situation. I don't think most solutions are that obvious."

"You may be right," Audrey acknowledged. "Remember though, something can be done and there is always something that you can do.

"When you don't know what to do, you have to create more options for yourself. When I'm in that situation, I use a simple exercise that has helped me create more options. Maybe this exercise will help you see more clearly when you're in the fog," Audrey suggested. "Write down the numbers 1 through 7 on a sheet of paper. Then start looking for at least 7 alternatives to your situation. Don't allow yourself to stop until you find at least 7. Consider possibilities that might seem 'out there.' Many times, you'll discover the best solution is the 7th one you wrote down – the one you had to rack your brain to come up with. It may also be helpful to ask others to come up with more options."

After writing Audrey's suggested exercise in his notes, Jack looked up. "Thanks for that tip. I'm already thinking of a few situations where I can use it."

"Great. I hope that helps," Audrey continued. "Worry is one of the two great fog-creating generators. The other is negative emotions. Successful people are positive people. Happy people are positive people. They find ways to duplicate situations when they were successful or happy, even though the current situation may be totally different. But less-successful people dwell on their past failures and many times wind up duplicating those failures.

"If you want to become your best, you have to sustain a positive, enthusiastic attitude. If you have a can-do attitude, you'll attract can-do people. Your attitude influences your approach to life and your relationships with others. It can be the catalyst to chart a new course for your life."

"You're not the first to mention this," Jack said. "Being positive has been a consistent theme among all my mentors on this journey."

"I thought it probably was," Audrey nodded. "Being positive is important. It matters. When you began your journey, you were probably not real enthusiastic. You were beaten down and unable to see things to be enthusiastic about. And that was probably obvious to everyone around you. The way you see things matters.

"I heard a story many years ago that reinforces my point:

"Two researchers working for a shoe manufacturer were independently dispatched to one of the world's least-developed countries. Their task was to evaluate the business potential within that country.

"After several weeks, a report came back from the first researcher, and the message read, 'No market here. Nobody wears shoes.' A few days later, the second report came back from the other researcher. It read, 'Great market here. Nobody wears shoes!'"

Audrey explained: "Those two people saw the same thing, but they saw it differently. The first guy would probably consider himself enthusiastic, but also a realist. Like many people, he fixated on one thing and could not see the bigger picture. In reality he was neither enthusiastic nor a realist. He couldn't see the opportunity because he was blinded by his perception of the obstacles in front of him.

"The second guy looked beyond the obvious and saw possibilities. He was focused on the opportunity that was crystal clear to him. Enthusiastic people see opportunity. Negative people can't see through their own fog to the potential right in front of them.

"Two other points to remember are: You have to assume control of what is controllable, and you get what you give."

Jack questioned: "I get the taking control of what is controllable, but what do you mean when you said I will get what I give?"

Then, Audrey related another story to make her point:

"Once there was a person who moved into a new town. He met a long-time resident and asked, 'I'm new to your town. What are the people like here?'

"'What were the people like in the town you came from?' the old-timer asked in return.

"'Well, they were pretty pessimistic and always complaining, and their glasses were always half-empty, never half-full,' the newcomer replied.

"'Hmmm,' said the old-timer. 'Sounds like the people who live here.'

"A few weeks later, another person moved to the same town and met the same old-timer. 'I'm new to your town. What are the people like here?' the newcomer asked.

"'What were the people like in the town you came from?' the old-timer asked again.

"'Well, they were terrific. We worked together in the neighborhood, helped each other out, and were always there to support each other during tough times. We're going to miss them now that we've moved,' the newcomer replied.

"'Hmmm,' said the old-timer. 'I think you'll like it here. That sounds about like the people who live here.'

"The old-timer's message? You get what you give. If you want to be around people who are positive, enthusiastic and eager to live life, your attitude has to be the same. If you think the people around you are glum and pessimistic, check yourself because that may be what you're reflecting, too. And, you control what you give."

Jack interrupted with an honest rebuttal. "But I have a hard time being enthusiastic when things are crashing all around me. I'd like to think I'm an enthusiastic person, but sometimes I fall off the enthusiasm wagon when the harsh reality of my situation takes over."

"Well, you're certainly not alone there," Audrey agreed. "Most people respond to negative events in a negative way, which is a natural and easier response. Being enthusiastic in the face of a negative event takes work. The naysayers and those comfortable with negative attitudes rationalize by saying they're being 'realistic.' In most cases, that means they refuse to even acknowledge a just-as-realistic positive response.

"Do you think your past has created a natural negative attitude?" Audrey wanted to know.

"Probably," Jack admitted.

Audrey nodded her head knowingly. "Unfortunately, we cannot change our past or the fact that people act in a certain way. Your attitude, however, is internally controlled. If you have a negative attitude, it's because you've made the choice to adopt a negative attitude.

"Fortunately, enthusiasm can be learned and developed. It's a choice you can make. It's up to you."

Jack latched on to Audrey's comment. "How can I learn to develop enthusiasm? Do you have some advice?"

Audrey quickly responded, "Enthusiasm may not come naturally to you. That's okay. Act enthusiastic. If you assume a trait, you will later possess it naturally. If you act enthusiastic, you will eventually become enthusiastic. First you seize it and then it will seize you. Your positive enthusiasm will become a way of life and will spread to those around you.

"One more thing about enthusiasm: Maintaining an enthusiastic outlook requires you to look for the best in yourself. Your self-image has a major impact on how you enjoy life. For instance, if you dwell on how unfair life is treating you, you will begin acting like a victim. You may perceive things that don't exist or give up because you think that nothing matters anyway. Ultimately your unfair perception can become your reality.

"Your enthusiasm for life begins with how you treat yourself. If you think about it, you're far more careful with what you say to others than with what you say to yourself. Typically, if you're like most, a large percent of your self-talk is negative – 'I can't, I won't, I'm not good enough,' etc. Your best friend would never use those discouraging words about you. And you would never talk to anyone else using the same negative words that you tell yourself.

"Even when you are stressed to the max, you need to talk to yourself like you would encourage your best friend. When you get discouraged, ask yourself what your best friend would say to you, and then say it to yourself. It will make a difference in how you feel about yourself, and in your ability to become the person you want to be.

"One last point, Jack. It's good to take the time to look around. You'll see that there are plenty of things to be thankful for, regardless of the challenge ahead of you. If you make it a point to list five things you're thankful for, and dwell on them for a few minutes every day, your attitude will improve immediately. Just five things. Taking a couple of minutes for gratitude, instead of concentrating on the things that annoy you, will change your life."

Jack listened carefully. Audrey's perspectives were helping him see his situation in a different light. He didn't want to leave but he realized his allotted time had elapsed. He told Audrey, "You've given me some great advice. You've helped me see that no one can lift my fog for me. I learned that regardless of what is going on, something can be done and the next move is mine. Also, I know that I'm not very kind when I talk to myself. I can do better in that area as well. Thank you for sharing your time and wisdom with me."

He then asked Audrey, "Is there anyone else you would suggest I talk to on my journey?"

"As a matter of fact, there is. One of my competitors for many years was Sam Campos. He taught me the value of providing outstanding service to my clients. You may want to get in touch with him. He's a good guy."

Jack was surprised by Audrey's suggestion. "I'll reach out to Sam. It's interesting that you respect a competitor so much that you'd send me his way. Thanks for the recommendation."

Audrey's Lessons:

Regardless of the situation, something can be done and there is something that I can do.

I have to lift my own fog.

It is up to me to turn off the powerful fog machines of worry and negative emotions.

I am wasting my time when I try to control the uncontrollable.

I have to maintain an enthusiastic attitude if I want to attract enthusiastic people around me.

I have to look for the best in myself.

I get what I give.

7

Be Great in Small Things

Jack could hardly wait to meet Sam Campos. Sam's organization was known as one of the best customer service providers in the nation. He was recognized throughout the region as a winner and had a reputation for winning with class.

When Jack arrived at Sam's office, he was amazed at the number of impressive awards on display. Three national publications' *Service Provider of the Year* awards for the previous year were prominently showcased. *If anyone knows something about success, it's this guy,* Jack thought to himself.

Sam greeted Jack in the reception area and escorted him to his office. Along the way, he took the time to introduce Jack to every employee they encountered. No one seemed to be intimidated by the owner walking around. In fact, they appeared to enjoy his presence. It was obvious Sam cared about his team and enjoyed a personal relationship with each of them, regardless of their role in the organization.

On the way to Sam's office, Jack noticed the saying: *'Be great in small things'* displayed in every hallway and office. *I bet that's Sam's most important principle,* he thought.

After settling into Sam's office and spending a few minutes getting to know each other, Jack asked his question, "Is there one principle you are convinced has contributed the most to your success?"

Sam began, "First, thank you for allowing me to participate in your research. I hope I'll be able to help. I enjoy talking about our team and what we do around here. Of course, I'm prejudiced, but I believe our people are the best.

"Many people look at our organization and believe we have something magical going on. They believe we're doing something that can't be duplicated. Actually, any organization can duplicate everything we do. It is very simple. Our motto and guiding principle is *Be great in small things.* We will provide every customer what they expect from us … and then, a little more."

"While we were walking toward your office, I noticed those words, *'Be great in small things'* throughout your hallways and workspaces," Jack commented. "It looks like you reinforce that principle everywhere."

"Absolutely. It's posted in every wing, hall and office," Sam responded. "It's our most important principle, and one we live every day. If every person on our team is great with the small things, the big things take care of themselves. Actually, it's a life principle.

"Adding a little more than is expected for our customers is what has separated us from our competitors. Rarely do people pay attention to normal. However, if you go just one step beyond normal, everyone takes notice. That's why being great in small things is so important to our success.

"By the way," Sam continued, "if you pay attention you can see many great people and organizations delivering 'great in small things' service. It's not something unique to us."

"Really?" Jack inquired. "I haven't seen any other organizations with the number of awards you display in your lobby. Would I recognize any of those great organizations?"

"Of course you would. As a matter of fact, here's an article I was reading right before you arrived. It is about an employee at Disney World." He picked up a magazine from his desk and passed it to Jack.

"Well, the article features an employee whose job is to clean guest rooms in a Disney hotel," Sam continued. "The story is about when she cleaned one guest room, not long ago, and she saw a newly purchased Mickey Mouse stuffed toy sitting in the corner. She did not leave it in the corner. When the family returned to their room, Mickey was sitting on the edge of the bed watching Disney cartoons on the television. Can you imagine what those kids thought when they saw Mickey watching television? The lady whose job it was to clean the room found a way to create happiness for that family. Was that magic? Of course not, but the exhausted kids who came in the room that evening thought so. Her small act will be talked about the rest of those kids' lives."

"Disney is a great service organization," Jack thought out loud. "They are successful and do a lot of things for their clients."

"Wait," Sam interrupted. "You missed the point. Disney does not teach employees to move stuffed toys to sit in front of a television. The cleaning lady could have left Mickey sitting in the corner, and she would have still done her job. But she didn't. She found a way to create happiness. My point is that everyone can be great in the small things, regardless of who you work for or what your role is in the organization."

"I see what you're saying. Everyone, including me, has an opportunity to be great in small things," Jack acknowledged.

"I'll bet you passed some 'great in small things' organizations on your way here," Sam said modestly. "Chick-fil-A is a good example. They are ultra-successful in an extremely competitive business. Their product is good, but it's not that much better than the other fast food restaurants. Their 'secret sauce' is not their food; it's the person you come in contact with when you order. It may even be the voice on the other end of the box when you drive through, or the person who comes to the drive-thru line with a menu, iPad, and smile, ready to personally take your order. Their 'great in small things' service makes you feel good about doing business with Chick-fil-A.

"Their success is not because of the chicken," Sam pointed out. "It's about being great in several small things. Have you noticed, for example, that every Chick-fil-A associate has been trained to say, 'My pleasure' after each transaction? That's a small thing that has become a major part of their differentiation."

"I have noticed. But do you really think they're so successful just because they say 'My pleasure?' I'm not so sure about that," Jack questioned.

Sam didn't seem surprised at Jack's hesitation and was ready to expand his premise. "I hear what you're saying. But let's think through what Chick-fil-A has to offer that is greater than any of the other fast food chains. Do they have substantially better food? Do they have a more comfortable place to eat? Is their drive-thru faster? Is their restaurant the cleanest? What do you think?"

"Well," Jack answered. "They're not really that different. Their food is good but not substantially better. The restaurants are not any more comfortable. In fact, I have to wait for a place to sit on most of my visits. The lines are long at the drive-thru. However, to their credit, my time in line is probably not much longer than at most other fast food places. They manage the drive-thru lines well and keep the lines moving. The restaurant is clean, but not substantially cleaner than other fast food places."

"So, why are the lines out the door?" asked Sam.

Jack pondered. "I guess because you feel good about eating there. And the reason you feel good is probably because you are guaranteed a smile from someone who acts like he or she cares about your business."

Sam continued. "There are plenty of chicken places. Unfortunately, it's not often that people who serve us actually tell us that it was their pleasure. In fact, in many places the customer is treated like an unwanted necessity. Simply saying 'My pleasure' reflects gratitude to the people who pay for their service. The Chick-fil-A employees do not treat their customer like it's their duty, obligation or burden to serve them. They are passionate about how they treat their customer. They have a desire, craving, and maybe even an obsession to treat you right.

"A simple truth is that people buy from people. When you are buying something, which type of person would you rather deal with? Someone who considers you a burden or someone who is obsessed about treating you right?"

"I want to do business with those who act like they like me," Jack responded.

"For sure you do," Sam agreed. "It may sound overly simple, but the greatest desire of employees and clients is to be appreciated. Chick-fil-A's philosophy is to 'Associate yourselves only with those people you can be proud of – whether they work for you or you work for them.' That's a small thing that creates a big gap between Chick-fil-A and their competitors.

"Chick-fil-A doesn't have exclusive rights on treating people well. For instance, Ritz Carlton is one of the best service organizations in the world because they recognize how important appreciating their guests and employees is to their success. Their operating philosophy is so simple that it's brilliant. Ritz's motto is 'We are Ladies and Gentlemen serving Ladies and Gentlemen.'"

"That is about as simple and profound as it gets," Jack responded. "I can see why they're so successful if they live that motto."

"They do." Sam added: "Being great in small things is among the best traits of the most successful organizations … and the most successful people. If you do more than what is required in any field, you will stand out from everyone else. Oh, for sure you have to be positive, knowledgeable, a problem solver and easy to do business with. But, more importantly, the most successful people are those that exhibit all of those traits, and then some.

"I have a friend, Phil Sloan, who is a great example of being great in small things," Sam continued. "Phil works at a club where I am a member. There are over 400 members in our club, and I assure you that every one of them can provide you personal examples of how Phil is great in the small things. He's one of the most amazing people I've ever known. He is so great in the small things that he's the gold standard for providing outstanding customer service. Phil takes a personal interest in me. He makes me feel terrific by asking about my family, texting and checking up on me when I haven't shown up at the club for a few weeks, continually asking if I need anything, and doing everything he can to make my life easier. His consistent actions reinforce that he cares about me."

"That is pretty impressive. What do you think has made him so great in small things?" Jack inquired.

Sam thought before responding. "I believe that some of it is because he is naturally friendly and has a servant's heart. He is also well trained, and he constantly reads. But he has a special talent. I think Phil's main attribute is that he loves his work. He once told me: 'I love going to work because I get to meet more new people every day.' I believe he's an example of how happiness at work begins before you leave home.

"Have you noticed how most people say they 'have to' go to work?"

"Sure," Jack responded. "Most people do have to go to work."

"Do they?" Sam asked. "I'm not against realizing your duty to make a living. But if you continually say you 'have to,' you sound like you're a victim and have no choice. I would be shocked if Phil ever woke up and told his wife Amy that he *had* to go to work, even though work is necessary to pay his bills. It may sound like a minor thing, but it's a negative way of looking at something important in your life. I bet as soon as Phil wakes up he tells Amy 'I *get* to go to work again!'

"I believe that to be successful, you have to be like Phil and love what you are doing. What if you changed your attitude from 'I *have to* go to work' to 'I *get to* go to work'? That one little change takes you away from being a victim and moves you toward acknowledging that work is a privilege. You'd be recognizing that you're grateful for having been provided the gift of work. It is a small thing, but this small thing can make a difference for you and those around you."

Jack contemplated what Sam had said. "I hadn't considered how my attitude toward going to work could impact my happiness or performance. That's an easy change to make. When I leave this meeting, I get to go to work again!"

Sam smiled and gave Jack a thumbs-up, then continued. "The '*being great in small things*' philosophy can add up to major improvements for you. If you add a little something extra every day and express gratitude in every transaction, it can change your life. The fact is that most people stop when they've done the minimum required. That's when adding 'the small things' begins."

"Is there any '*being great in small things*' activity that you try to do every day?" Jack asked.

"That's a good question." Sam smiled as he pulled out a stack of personalized notes. "See these notes? I write at least one personal note to an employee or customer every day. It takes me about five minutes, but it's some of the best time I spend.

You'd be surprised how often people remember a short note I sent them."

"I'm not surprised," Jack said. "I have received complimenting emails, but I've never written or received a note like that out of the blue. Others may think writing a personal note is no big deal, but if I were to receive one, it would be extremely meaningful."

"Complimenting people through emails is good but there is no substitution for a personal handwritten note," Sam continued. "There are other terrific examples of actions taken by people who are great in the small things. For instance, making a personal call to encourage someone has a far greater impact than leaving a voicemail or sending a text or email. Or remembering facts about a customer, like a birthday or significant family events, will separate you from your competitors. Or, if you show up at a meeting fully prepared and armed with the research required to make a decision. Or if you volunteer for a project. You would be doing the small things that most people ignore. Those are a just a few examples; there are many more small things you can do that would be meaningful. Don't make it complicated, because it's not. Your employer and customers will become loyal to you if you develop an urgency in being great in the small things. They'll be glad to keep doing business with you.

"My goal is to provide more than what others expect from me or my team. I tell our team that going the extra mile is not nearly as hard as finishing the scheduled race. There are not many people traveling the extra mile and you may find yourself alone – but that's where lasting success happens.

"I think the major key to my accomplishments has been the attitude of '*being great in small things*.' It doesn't matter if you call it the extra mile, my pleasure, or being ladies and gentlemen serving ladies and gentlemen – what *does* matter is that you reflect what you want to reflect."

"It almost sounds too simple," Jack whispered under his breath.

"I agree," Sam said, hearing Jack's whisper. "It's simple. Do what is expected and then some. If you are willing to do more than you are paid to do, eventually you will be paid more to do what you do. When you reach that point, you will be among the best. I am living proof. It may be a simple principle, but it requires that you commit to pay the price to be better than average."

Jack observed, "Herb Hill introduced me to the say/do ratio. He says we should never commit to more than we are able to deliver. You're suggesting that we should do what we say we will … and then some more. That would definitely set me apart from the average person. You're both in agreement, but you add '*being great in small things*.'"

"Exactly," Sam acknowledged. "There is no magical formula to success. My most significant moment was discovering the power of the small things. Other people have discovered their 'aha' moment in different places. Regardless of when and where you experience your aha moment, your success will require a combination of good choices, some of which are seemingly insignificant.

"I suggest you continue your visits. Go visit my friend Cal LeBlanc. I'll call him and 'grease the skid' for you. I think he has figured out success pretty well. But I'll give you a fair warning – don't let his modesty fool you. He is one of the most successful people I have ever known."

"I've heard he has an inquiring mind. I look forward to meeting him." Jack thanked Sam for his time and immediately wrote down his thoughts from the meeting.

Sam's Lessons:

Achieving success is not magical. It requires moving beyond the average and doing more than what was in my job description when I was hired.

My success is not about my 'chicken.' Success begins with people feeling great about themselves when they are around me because I give them a little something extra.

Not many people travel the extra mile. That is where success is.

If I want to be the best, I have to do what is expected and then some.

I need to be great in small things.

8

Ask Why

While driving to meet Cal LeBlanc, Jack reflected on everything he'd learned in the past few weeks. He realized how fortunate he was to learn about success from people in his community. *Each person I've visited has given me simple suggestions,* he thought. *Don't I need a more complicated, defined strategy to achieve success? I expected to learn secret strategies, but each person I've talked to so far has focused on sharing his or her very simple philosophies. Am I missing something? Maybe Cal has a specific strategy he will share with me.*

Cal LeBlanc owned several small businesses in the community. He was active in the local civic organizations and was on the school board. He seemed to know almost everyone in town. Jack could hardly wait to meet him.

Jack and Cal had agreed to meet at Cal's home on Saturday morning. When Jack arrived, Cal greeted him at the door and led him to his impressive office. Lining the office walls were pictures of Cal with some of the most influential people in the state, and his bookcase was loaded from floor to ceiling with books and memorabilia. To the left of the bookcase was an impressive vintage Italian globe on a black wooden stand. Jack was impressed. It was a cool place to meet.

Cal showed Jack around and asked about Jack's personal life, his success journey and his background. After a few minutes, they settled into soft, comfortable leather chairs.

Cal then asked Jack how he could help.

Jack explained he was seeking to learn how to reboot himself. He filled Cal in on the lessons he'd learned in the previous stops on his journey, and then asked his question, "Is there something unique you think has contributed to your success?"

"Before I answer your question, why are you on this journey?" Cal asked.

"Well," Jack replied, "I'm probably no different than most. I want to be my best and become successful. I want to know how to get there."

"But, why do you want to become successful?" Cal asked. "You know there's a price to be paid for success – and that price isn't cheap, either."

"Sure. If it were easy, I would already have it," Jack said defensively. "I want to become successful so I can provide for my family and give back to my community. I also want to help others reach their potential. I really want success more for what I can do with it than what it will do for me."

Cal interrupted. "Forgive my suspicious nature, but that sounds like a soundtrack you rehearsed before you came here. But I'll take you at your word. So, if you find success, what changes will you make in your life? To use your words, 'what are you going to do with it?'"

Jack pulled out a list of his goals and went over each goal with Cal. Jack proudly shared his professional, financial, spiritual and physical goals. Each goal included an action plan with his anticipated result.

"That is impressive," said Cal. "Most people don't have goals. Those who do, have not written them down with a plan to achieve them. People like you who write down their goals in concrete terms are far more likely to attain them. I can already tell you're not just another average person."

Jack stopped Cal. "I must admit to you, before I began this journey, I didn't have any specific goals, much less any written down. Maybe if I had taken goal-setting seriously, my journey wouldn't have been necessary. But every person I have visited has reinforced the importance of goals and living with purpose. That's why I now have specific goals. It is probably one of the most important things I've learned from talking to everyone, so far."

"Well, that's even more impressive," Cal said. "You paid attention and now you're making some significant changes. What process are you using for your goal-setting?"

"That's great question," Jack answered. "I have a 'before' and an 'after' answer. Before my visits on this journey, I didn't have a process to achieve anything. When I asked myself: '*What are my goals?*' My answer was, '*I don't know.*' After several visits, I came to realize what Brad Harris meant when he referred to 'drifting without purpose.' My revelation was that I didn't clearly understand what success was to me, so how could I do the things that would get me where I wanted to go?"

Cal nodded. "That is a huge, important discovery. The tragedy for most people isn't that they don't achieve their goals, it's that they have not established any goals to reach. Not having specific goals allowed you to keep your expectations low and protect yourself from disappointment. That's what may have led you to where you were when you began your journey – stuck! So, what did you do?"

"Well, as you said, I paid attention," Jack confirmed. "Each person I talked to had achieved long-term success by making deliberate decisions and conscious efforts toward specific goals they were trying to accomplish. They knew exactly what they wanted. It was specific, measurable and attainable. I had to get serious about knowing how to set goals if I was ever going to achieve them."

"So, what else did you do?" Cal wanted to know.

"I went and talked to a person I have respected for years, my college golf coach," Jack smiled.

"Well, that's a twist." Cal was now especially curious. "I am sure you made his day when you sought his advice. What did you learn?"

Jack was pleased to answer. "I have been doing a lot of reflection, I realized that when I was a student I had specific and measurable goals. My coach was the person who taught me the value of having specific goals. But somewhere along the way, I quit using the goal-setting process that he had taught me. So, I went to him for a refresher.

"Interestingly, my coach taught me that my goals in life should follow the same process as my golf routine," Jack shared. "Regardless of my goal, I have to see, feel, trust and do if I want to achieve anything significant. He taught me to create my goal four times in four different ways:

> "**First, I see the goal** in a mental picture. I visualize it as a positive situation – what I want to happen, rather than fearing what I don't want to happen. *For example, if I want to lose twenty pounds, I visualize myself weighing 180 lbs. I begin thinking how it feels to weigh 180 and what difference it makes in my life to be at that weight.*

> "**Second, I feel it** when I write down the goal. Writing the goal on paper and describing it in positive and personal terms, and in the present tense, clarifies exactly what I want to accomplish. *I would write down 'I weigh 180 on June 12.'*

> "**Third, I trust it** when I tell others. I share with people who will support me and hold me accountable. It's important for me to trust my decision to achieve the goal and tell others because it holds me accountable to someone other than myself and helps me move forward. And, hopefully, I can bring another person on the trip with me. *I tell them I will weigh 180 on June 12 and ask them to hold me accountable at several benchmarks along the way.*

> "**Fourth, I do it** when I take action toward the goal. I begin with a plan that includes:

- My honest assessment of my current situation. *I currently weigh 200.*

- My deadline to accomplish the goal. *On June 12 I weigh 180.*

- The anticipated obstacles I have to overcome. *I have to change my eating habits, including how often I go out, who I go out with, and the type of foods that I eat. I also need to drink more water and less alcohol.*

- A list of the people whose help I will need. *My wife, peers and associates need to be my encouragers.*

- My plan to accomplish the goal. *I begin tracking calories and limit myself to 2,000 calories a day. Exercise more and walk at least 10,000 steps a day.*

- Finally, I make a list, in order of priority, that includes what I have to do in order to make my goal a reality.

"That example is simple, but the same process works with all my personal and professional goals. See, feel, trust and do. It's like a recipe – if I leave out a step or an ingredient, I'm not going to get the result I want."

Cal was impressed. "That's good stuff. Why do you need to write your goals down or tell others? Why not just go to the 'do it' phase?"

"I had the same question," Jack acknowledged, "but I committed myself to trying the full process. I discovered that when I wrote my goals on paper, it clarified my thoughts. Sometimes it's difficult for me to 'see' my goals vividly in my mind, but when I write my thoughts on paper it's difficult to be vague."

"In addition to clarifying the goal, writing it down forces me to answer two important questions: Is the goal worthwhile and is this goal attainable? If the answer is 'no' to either of these questions, I need to rethink my goal.

"Then, obviously, I have to do it. My goals are now a part of my life. I have posted them on my mirror at home, as a screensaver in my home office and on my desk at work, and I have a laminated card listing my goals in my wallet. They are visible everywhere I go. I am finally realizing it's not helpful to come up with great goals and then stash them away and check back on my progress a year later. I now work on my goals every day."

"That is impressive," Cal exclaimed. "This alone can be a game-changer for you. You're absolutely right when you say the most difficult thing is to clearly understand what you want, but it's also the most important thing. The same goal-setting process applies in all areas of your life. If you focus on improving each of those areas, you'll discover they all get stronger. I was happy to hear you talk about all four areas today.

"You are making real progress!" Cal continued. "I understand you've visited a lot of people already. So, why did you come to me?"

Jack responded, "I'm here to learn from you. I have visited several people already and every person provided me some great suggestions. Sam said you would be another good resource for me. The question I've been asking everyone, and now I ask you is: What is the most important principle you believe has contributed to your success?"

"That is a good question," Cal said with a laugh. "I love questions. But before I answer, let me tell you about some of my observations. I have seen many people approach success as a zero-sum game. They believe if they are successful at work, it prevents them from being successful at home. They believe if they spend time on their physical health, it takes away from their spiritual health. Those are myths. That is simply not true. The most successful people are balanced. They work hard but they do not sacrifice their family, finances, spirituality or physical health.

"In fact, I think you can only be genuinely successful when you pay close attention to each of those areas. They are interdependent and all affect your life. Your work will be better if you have a healthy body, a compassionate soul, and you feed your mind with new and positive ideas. Your home life will be better if you enjoy your work. Your work and home success are connected with each other.

"Regardless of your financial results, you will not experience success if you lose your family, health or compassion. You have to integrate your work with the rest of your life. You don't measure success by money – you will never have the most money. Success is measured by how well you become the very best version of you.

"I can tell that you're serious about finding success because you have identified good reasons for finding it."

"Thanks for your encouragement, but I'm here to learn from you," said Jack.

"Well, you might have picked up on my unique success principle, if you think about it." Cal smiled and then continued. "It's simple – *Ask Why*. That was my most important discovery – simply ask why. I observed many people cannot answer the question of *why* they are doing what they are doing. They get stuck doing the same things over and over without taking the time to ask why they're doing them or understand why it's important that they be done.

"I learned a long time ago, if people understood why things are the way they are, they could adjust to almost anything. Success eludes many people because they do not have a clear plan to allow it to happen. Then, when they achieve a level of success, they don't know how to handle it. You are several steps ahead of most people searching for success. You have already asked yourself *why* and are now asking others *how*."

"Thanks. This goal-setting process is new to me. I'm definitely a work in progress," Jack admitted.

"It seems to me," Cal, a connoisseur of questions, interjected, "that one of the most important questions you can ask is, 'What do you think?' That's why you are asking me and other people in our community about success. You've acknowledged you may not know, and others may have the answers. To be successful, you don't need to know everything. You just need to fill in the gaps of what you are missing as quickly as you can.

"In addition, I have found that, most of the time, the answers are close by. If it's a business question, your peers will probably have the answer, if you ask them. If your question is about something at home, your spouse probably has the answer, if you have the courage to admit you don't know and ask what they think.

"I believe your success is not very far away. It is close." Cal paused and then offered, "I suggest you visit my friend, Lindy Marsalis; he may be able to add a piece to your success puzzle."

"Wait!" Jack exclaimed. "I was hoping you'd be able to provide me a strategy. I thought that you would recommend specific actions I could take to ensure my success. I'm not sure that asking why is an actionable strategy for me to implement."

After listening, Cal asked, "Why do you think there is already a strategic success plan written for you? What have all of your other visits taught you?"

Jack pondered for a minute and then responded. "I didn't think that a strategic success plan would be written and revealed to me. But I assumed that success was more than just doing some of the basic things I've learned on my journey. I guess one of the things I'm learning is that everything begins with my attitude that I can be successful. Then, I have to develop a strong desire to pay the price for success.

"Reflecting on my previous visits, I think I now understand why I fell into the rut I've been in for a while. It was because I did not realize *why* it's important to blast through tough, hug change and avoid drifting. I never considered *why* saluting the truth, protecting my integrity or being great in small things mattered.

"I didn't realize it until you asked me *why* so many times. Now, I understand *what* and *why*. None of those principles alone will become my plan. But, if I leave even one of them out of my strategy, it will prevent me from becoming the person I want to be."

Jack paused and gathered his thoughts. "I guess I answered my own question. Your question of 'why' is maybe the most important question I can answer about myself," he said almost apologetically.

"Now, I'll take your advice and visit Lindy Marsalis to see if he can add another piece to my success puzzle."

As Jack left Cal, he realized with amazement that almost the entire conversation had focused on answering Cal's questions. It had been an enlightening experience.

For the first time Jack understood the power of asking why.

Cal's Lessons:

No one can create my success plan for me.

Asking myself 'why' helps to clarify if the price required for success is worthwhile.

Success is not a zero-sum game. Becoming my very best involves being successful in each area of my life.

I don't need to know everything. I just need to fill in the gaps of what I am missing as fast as I can.

Ignoring any of the previous principles shared by each of the successful people will derail my success.

Visit Where Luck Lives

As he left Cal's home, Jack was deep in thought. *I hadn't considered my journey as a puzzle before Cal mentioned it*, he said to himself. *Maybe that's how I should have been thinking all along. There is not one magical answer ... all the answers fit together. Without doing what each person has told me, I will never be my best. Cal may have revealed what I need to do by making me answer why so often.*

It was time for Jack to follow Cal's suggestion and meet Lindy Marsalis. Jack had heard that a lot of people around town called him Lucky Lindy because everything he touched seemed to turn to gold. *Maybe Lindy will give me some new insights on how to get lucky*, he thought to himself.

Jack drove over to Lindy's office, where they'd agreed to meet. At six-foot-five, Lindy towered over him, and his rugged good looks, confidence and poise gave him an intimidating presence. Lindy extended his hand, which Jack figured was as big as a bear paw, and then flashed a glowing, contagious smile. He was dressed casually but smartly in jeans and a sport coat. There was something special about Lindy's smile and the way he presented himself that immediately offset his initial intimidating presence.

"Greetings, Jack. I have heard so much about you. Welcome. Please excuse me while I clear off my desk. I was just reading a most interesting book – one I plan to give to every member of my team. It opened my eyes to some things I once knew but forgot somewhere along the way."

Lindy closed the book and offered Jack a seat nearby. "I understand you've been asking a lot of questions from several of my peers. How can I help?"

"Yes, sir. It's been quite a trip," Jack acknowledged. "I'm here because I believe you may hold another piece to my success puzzle. Cal LeBlanc recommended I visit you. I'm sure you've earned your 'lucky' nickname. I want to get lucky, too. I hope you will share with me your thoughts about luck and your success secrets."

"Well, I hope I can help a little," Lindy began. "When I reflect over my career, my success involved a combination of several events … and a little luck didn't hurt. However, luck wasn't the driving factor. The events that helped me were created by my choices – sometimes difficult and uncomfortable choices. When all of the choices were woven together, eventually that led me to accomplishing my goals.

"Successful people struggle making difficult choices, the same as everyone else. The difference is that they don't quit. Their goals are so vivid in their minds, they realize the result they will accomplish is worth the price of a difficult choice.

"Regarding luck, a lot of people are confused about luck," Lindy continued. "A lot of people who are disappointed with their level of achievement are convinced that other people's success is simply a matter of good luck. Many assume their lack of success is because of bad luck. They believe luck painstakingly searches for a fortunate few to bestow good fortune upon them.

"Luck doesn't track you down. Actually, the opposite is true … you must conscientiously seek out luck and go where luck is. You can't just want, hope or wish for luck to show up. You must actively track it down."

Jack interjected. "That makes sense, but where do you track down luck? There is no map that says, 'Find luck here.'"

"Of course, there aren't any luck maps. People would like for luck to show up on demand or have Siri provide the directions to take them to it. They want an instant, spontaneous combustion of success. The truth is, you have to meet luck where it is and there is no spontaneous combustion of luck. You have to ignite the fire."

Lindy leaned forward to make sure he had Jack's undivided attention. "Listen very closely. This is important. Luck lives in knowledge. It only shows up where knowledge is present. The way to create your own luck is to increase your knowledge.

"My success secret is very simple, *Visit where Luck Lives, Increase my Knowledge and Get Lucky!* Knowledge is the power that closes the gap between your potential and your performance. The more you learn, the luckier you will be."

"That makes sense, I guess," Jack reasoned. "I've been out of school for quite a while and increasing my knowledge has not been at the top of my to-do list for years. What can I do at this stage in my life to learn more and become luckier?"

Lindy was quick to respond again. "Most people assume their education concluded when they graduated. There is nothing further from the truth. After graduation is when your most meaningful education commences. Separating the most successful people from others is knowledge – mostly learned long after attending their last class.

"Successful people are zealous about their personal growth. They are okay with exiting a comfortable place and entering into an unknown space that, many times, becomes their launching pad. You see, every time you move through an exit, you enter into a new opportunity. The only way for you to go through the entrance into the next level of your career is for you to exit your current level. That's what creating luck does – it uses the power of knowledge to exit the status quo and enter into a new beginning.

"Think about when you started your success journey. When you began asking others what contributed to their success, did your knowledge improve? Was your thinking challenged? Were you surprised at some of the answers to your question?"

"Yes, to all of the above," Jack admitted.

"The reason why you're closer to success now than you've ever been before is that you have more knowledge. You uncovered the most important piece of your puzzle before you came to see me. You found out, maybe without even realizing it, that knowledge is power. The more you learn, the more valuable you become to those around you.

"Think about it. Why did you search out Ashley, Brad, Cal and all the others?"

"Because," Jack said, "they had been where I am trying to go."

Lindy stood up, put his hands on his desk, leaned forward and looked Jack squarely in the eyes. Then he firmly but kindly made his point. "Exactly. People search out those who have learned the most. Every one of your visits was to a person who had some knowledge you were seeking. Learning from them is the fuel you need to ignite your inner fire to become the person you want to be.

"Preparing for success is not easy," Lindy continued. "It's hard work requiring a detailed plan. You have to allocate expenses and resources, and provide an accounting of your results. You also have to remain somewhat fluid to adjust to changing conditions. The most important part of your success plan preparation is to increase your knowledge.

"To increase your knowledge, you can build your own learning experiences. You are today what you'll be in the future, except for the people you meet and the learning experiences you create. You can be completely different or just like you are right now – it is your choice," Lindy reinforced his point. "Think about that. Completely different ... or the same as you are today. So, think back. How do you compare to who you were five years ago?"

Jack was not excited about the answer he was about to give. "Back then, I had no idea I would be trying to figure out what success would look like five years forward. But, here I am. I haven't made much progress, if any. I didn't have a plan." He paused. "I may not be as well off today as I was five years ago. That is sobering."

Lindy was quick to encourage. "Everyone you have visited on your journey has come to the same solemn realization that something had to change for them to become the person they wanted to be. The change most made was to increase their knowledge faster and be careful to not allow obstacles to prevent their knowledge from expanding. Don't feel sorry for yourself. There's no time for whining. It's time for you to paint a vivid picture in your mind of who you want to be in five years and begin brushing your own canvas. You can begin making your vision a reality today.

"The beauty of increasing your knowledge is that you don't have to leave your desk to get started. The book I was reading when you arrived is also available to you or anyone else, if they had been seeking it. Knowledge is more available today than it has ever been in history, but it still will not come looking for you … you have to search for it. Don't stifle your career by limiting your knowledge."

"What do you suggest?" Jack wanted to know.

"I'm glad you asked." Lindy was obviously passionate about this subject. "Knowledge is a gift received only by persistent people, because only they will do what is needed to find it. Unlucky people never go looking for knowledge. It's up to you to go where luck is and use the information that is there. Luck resides in knowledge. Let me repeat – *luck resides in knowledge*. One new idea has the power to transform your life forever, but you must have more knowledge to try new ideas.

"A lot of people say that I am lucky," Lindy continued. "I agree. However, I don't agree with most of those people on *why* I've been so fortunate. They believe luck just consistently gets in my way and I can't even avoid it. Ha! I wish that were the case. Nothing could be further from the truth.

"Luck does not jump into my path any more than it does yours," Lindy confessed. "I think the reason I'm lucky is because I live my life by my choices, not by chance. I made a conscious decision many years ago that I would not allow my future to be determined by chance, which is unpredictable, uncontrollable, coincidental and unplanned. I don't think that's a good way to live, and it's certainly not a good way to achieve long-term success."

Jack reflected on his own situation and then said, "Looking back, obviously my choices have not been that great. What type of choices have helped you become lucky?"

Lindy gathered his thoughts before responding. "Well, to begin with, I choose not to be a victim, regardless of how unfair I may think a situation is. I choose to commit to my goals. I choose to live my values with integrity, overcome adversity, develop positive relationships and leave a legacy for those who will follow me. Each of those decisions is specific and important to my success.

"If I'd just waited for luck to find me, I would never have accumulated the knowledge I needed to be successful. My luckiest moment was when a respected peer suggested I make the choice to pursue knowledge – and then take my chances. It has worked out well for me."

"That was a wise peer and friend," Jack agreed. "Specifically, what do you recommend I do?"

Lindy was quick with his recommendation. "Invest in yourself. Most people don't make that investment, but it is the most powerful and effective success tool you can use.

"Here's my challenge to you: Read one book a month that will help you grow personally or professionally. During the next year, you'll have read 12 books. When the next job opening at a higher position comes up, would you be better prepared to assume that role because of that knowledge? Of course you would. You, too, would be lucky.

"Think of what accepting my challenge could mean to you. Average people do not read one nonfiction book in a year. Not one. However, a common trait among executives is that they are avid readers. Many top executives read several books a month, yet average employees might not read five non-fiction books in their lifetime after completing their formal education. That's not a coincidence. Those executives understand that reading helps them see more alternatives, think more clearly, and make better decisions.

"How long do you think it will be before you retire?" Lindy's question seemed to come out of left field.

"Unless I get really lucky, I'll retire in 15 years or so. It may take me a little longer, but my best guess is 15 years," Jack answered.

Lindy smiled. "Think about this. You could read 180 books in 15 years if every day you read half a chapter, which would take about 10 minutes. That will make an incredible difference in your career, your life and for those around you. And it will provide you a much more rewarding and fulfilling retirement. I am living proof that the more you learn, the more you earn. You can, too."

Jack pushed back. "But I'm not a big reader. It's not something I enjoy. I prefer to listen to audios, watch and listen to podcasts, or watch TED Talks."

"That's fine," Lindy acknowledged. "I encourage you to create your own learning experience, but you retain more knowledge when you read, underline, and touch the pages of a book than you do watching or listening to someone speak. A better suggestion is to do both. Read for 10 minutes a day and there's still plenty of time for any other learning experience you want to create. It's easy to agree you need to become a lifelong learner. But nothing is going to change unless you shift into creating your own luck right where you are. It's a choice available to you right now.

"One more thing. Positive people tend to attract luck like a magnet. It pulls people toward them. On the other hand, I have never known a lucky person who was negative and cynical. Never. Not once in my career have I met that person. I don't think that is an accident. If you're like me, you probably prefer to surround yourself with positive, energetic and enthusiastic people."

Jack agreed. "I don't like to be around negative and cynical people, either. They tend to drag me down with them."

Lindy picked up on Jack's comment. "You're right. They will drag you down if you allow them. The people around you will have a huge impact on how positive or negative you will be. Be careful whom you choose to spend your time with."

Lindy's tone was serious. "Be aware. You can tell a lot about the direction a person's life is heading by watching the people whom they choose to spend time with. More likely than not, you will become eerily similar to the people whom you hang around with. That can be a blessing or a curse. You need to be around people who bless you, not curse you. That is a decision you control."

Jack looked back at his notes, smiled and said, "I had never put too much thought into evaluating whom I surround myself with until Brad told me the exact same thing. He, too, said I would most likely become like the people I spend the most time with."

Lindy was not surprised. "It's the truth. Most people want optimistic and enthusiastic people around them, but it takes effort. It is like the flu. If you want to catch the flu, go where people have the flu. Anytime you want to catch something, go where it already is. Are you surrounding yourself with positive, helpful, hopeful people? If you are, you'll have a lot more reasons to remain positive, helpful and hopeful yourself. That's a choice you can make."

Jack didn't agree with Lindy's assessment, so he took a minute to frame his words carefully before responding. "That's good in theory, but I don't get to choose some of the people I have to be around. I deal with customers, employees and even some family members who are not blessings to me all the time."

Lindy was ready with his response. "Yes, of course everyone has to tolerate people who occasionally are not blessings. But you can choose to not allow them to pull you down. You can choose to not accept their negativity and cynicism. You control your own actions.

"To attract positive people, you must act positive," Lindy instructed. "To attract successful people, you must act successful. The people whom you attract will influence the person you become. If you want to be a positive, committed, successful person, it will be difficult to become that person if you continually surround yourself with negative, lukewarm, whining people."

He looked up at the clock on his wall. "Well, I see we're almost out of time, but I want you to know … I am grateful you came to visit with me. You're on a good track. Keep moving. Remember, make knowledge an intentional daily habit. The more knowledge you have, the more respect, freedom, happiness and success you will earn! You will become more valuable to those around you. And, as you are aware, people seek out those who have learned the most. That is how you can become lucky, make better choices, and learn more to earn more."

Lindy paused before he continued. "I'm going to suggest you visit one more person, a friend of mine named Grace Laymance. I think she'll be able to provide you with another piece of your success puzzle."

"I'll seek out Grace," Jack promised. "Thank you for your time, Lindy. You have provided me great wisdom. Luck lives in knowledge. That's where I need to spend more time. I won't wait around for luck to find me."

Lindy's Lessons:

To get lucky, I have to go where luck is … and luck lives in knowledge.

I live my life by my choices, not by chance.

I am today what I will be in the future, except for the people I meet and the learning experiences I create.

If I want to attract positive people, I have to stay positive.

10

Do Something at Once

Jack's journey was nearing completion. His final stop was to visit with Grace Laymance, a professor at the state university. Grace had enjoyed a stellar career in business before she decided to pursue her passion of teaching. She lived an hour away from Jack, so they agreed to meet on a Saturday morning at Grace's home.

When Jack arrived, she welcomed him and invited him into her den, which also functioned as her study. It was immaculate and fashionable. Her endearing Golden Labrador Retriever nestled close to the blazing fire in the fireplace. A couple of walls in the room were decorated with pictures of her family. Another wall was a bookcase packed with books and memorabilia. It was a warm, comfortable setting.

Grace was eager to hear about Jack's previous visits. He filled her in on his experience and the lessons he had learned thus far. Then, Grace began. "I'm impressed. You are one of the very few people to invest the time, energy and effort to correct your path and seek improvement. Most people wait around for things to get better and then wonder why things remain the same. Congratulations on taking the initiative to proactively enrich your life."

"Thanks for your kind words. It's been interesting, revealing and life changing," Jack said with a smile. "Each meeting has elevated my awareness of what I need to do to be the person I want to become. I've heard a lot of good things about you, and I'm eager to hear about a defining moment that led to your thoughts about achieving success."

"I'm glad you're here," Grace said. "Actually, right now you're doing what became my most important belief about achieving success. I'm sure you were tempted to delay or even cancel your journey. You may have been afraid of where it would take you. You had to gather a great deal of courage to call and meet with people that you didn't know. Most people would have found a reason to postpone their journey until a more convenient time, a time that would probably have never come."

"I did put off this journey a long time," Jack admitted. "Unfortunately, I began my search only after I had reached my wit's end."

Grace smiled and continued. "It took me quite a while to learn that putting things off was keeping me from getting where I wanted to go. I postponed pursuing my passion of teaching and mentoring others for several years before I left the business world. Procrastinating was my best friend. I think it's many people's closest associate. I was no different than all the other people who seem to love to procrastinate.

"Then, one day I read where Calvin Coolidge stated, 'We cannot do everything at once, but *we can do something at once!*' That statement stuck with me. I can do something at once. There is no need to wait around to get started. That changed my perspective. My defining moment was when I discovered that I could 'do something at once!' That is also what you have done by embarking on your own success journey."

Jack admitted, "I wish I'd had the wisdom to turn my back to procrastination. I think I made it my best friend until I couldn't go any longer. I wish..."

"Hey, you're here," Grace interrupted. "Do you see anyone else around here? Did you meet anyone else on their own journey? Did any of the other people you contacted tell you to 'get in line?' No. There was no one waiting in line. You turned your back on procrastination when you made your first call to Vince Garrett.

"Rather than moving forward into an unfamiliar or uncomfortable new area, many people habitually return to Someday Isle. That's where procrastination lives, too. It's named after all the people who continually put things off. *Someday I will*, or *someday I'm going to*, are the rallying cries of the residents of Someday Isle. Never in history has a situation improved on its own while people sat basking in the sun, doing nothing on Someday Isle."

Grace leaned forward and firmly reassured Jack. "You are not on Someday Isle; you are right here! You are doing well."

"I appreciate your encouragement," Jack said. "What advice can you give me about 'do something at once?' Do you have any specific suggestions to move past procrastinating?"

Grace assembled her thoughts and then began teaching. "Absolutely. One of my core beliefs is that *you own your time*. It is for you to spend any way you see fit. Finding a reason to put off doing what needs to be done is always an option available to you. Don't allow yourself to take that option any longer. I know people who, unknowingly, are at their most creative when they're thinking of reasons why it's okay to delay doing something that needs to be done. They are too busy, too bored, too old, too young, too stressed, too comfortable – their excuses run on and on. That is not a great way to live. They will never see their possibilities or reach their potential. Success will only come to those whose actions rise above their excuses … just like you have on your journey."

Jack chimed in with a quick question: "So, how can I avoid the procrastination trap? Maybe I have allowed it to become a habit for me."

"That's a good question. Get ready. This is my favorite subject." Jack could tell that Grace was delighted to share her knowledge.

"Since you own your time, you have to *assume control of your situation*. One of the major sources of stress, anxiety and unhappiness comes from feeling like your life is out of your control. You need to discern how to take control of your time so you can take control of your life. Your time is your responsibility; no one else can accept that responsibility for you. You are the only one who can make adjustments to solve that problem."

Jack listened and then asked, "How can I figure out how to take control of my time and my life? A lot of things are beyond my control."

"Sure, some things are beyond your control," Grace agreed "However, you probably have more control than you're giving yourself credit for. If you're like most people, you may wait around for all the stars to be aligned before you do anything. ***Quit waiting around for the perfect time to get something done.*** You may never have as much information as you would like, but you have to seize the moment, courage up, and make the best decision you can. If you waited for the perfect situation, you would never get married, get promoted, have kids, or make any major decisions. There is no such thing as the perfect time. You will not get much of anything done unless you go ahead and do something before the timing is completely perfect. The key is that you have to 'do something at once.' Do something to take your first step off Someday Isle. Taking a small step is far better than planning some giant leaps that are never taken."

Grace emphatically continued. "Also, ***evaluate if your task has to be done perfectly.*** I've seen many people with good intentions get bogged down trying to do things perfectly, when perfect was not worth the time or effort. Perfection paralysis is expensive. It costs you time, energy, emotions and money. And it prevents you from doing other important things. There is no good reason to spend more time than is necessary on things that simply don't require it.

"Procrastination is a frustrating habit. You have to consciously attack it by having the mindset that ***there is no better time to get things done than right now.***"

"Hold on." Jack wanted clarification. "What about gathering all the facts so that you can make a better decision?"

Grace quickly responded, "Procrastination doesn't begin until you have enough facts available to move forward. It begins when you delay action after you have the necessary information to move forward. When you have enough information, *putting things off rarely improves your decision*. In fact, realizing you have something to do that should have already been done just increases your stress.

"It may sound elementary, but to confront procrastination, you need to *consistently create a to-do list … and then do something*. The anxiety and dread you have about what needs to be done rapidly declines when you have a specific plan. Write down what needs to be done and give yourself a deadline. If there is a task you especially dislike, do it first, then move down your list. One of the best questions you can ask yourself is: *If I could accomplish only one thing right now, what would that one thing be?* Your answer will quickly identify where you should be directing your attention."

"Yeah," Jack interjected, "but what about when you're responsible for a big task – one that you can't just 'do something at once' and be done with it?" He sincerely wanted to know.

"I understand," Grace said carefully. "Sometimes the task seems too daunting to even get started. If that's the case, *break it down into smaller pieces* and hold yourself accountable for at least getting one piece done today, another one tomorrow, etc. The hardest step you'll take to get something done is to *get started*. You'll be a lot happier if you 'do something at once' and have a steady stream of minor accomplishments, rather than waiting to complete one major project.

"An enemy of 'do something at once' is fear. One way to combat your fear is to ask yourself, *'How will I feel if I do nothing?'* There's a cost for doing nothing and you may find that price is not worth paying."

Jack was quick to agree. "Sometimes I don't want to get started because, subconsciously, I don't want to finish. I think I may enjoy having some things on my to-do list."

"Believe me," Grace responded, "you will always have something on your to-do list that needs to be done. What you need to reconcile is the question of 'are the important things getting done?'

"'Do something at once' does not mean that everything needs to be done. You may need to **eliminate things that do not need to be done at all**. Ask yourself, 'Can I say no to some of those things and free myself up to work on more important things?' Truthfully answering that question may be the best way to find out what actually needs to be done."

Grace continued. "'Do something at once' requires you to **be decisive**. When someone says, 'Call me later and set an appointment,' respond with, 'Let's save ourselves a call and make the appointment now.' Then it's done and you don't have to make another call just to arrange a meeting.

"My last tip about 'doing something at once' is to face conflicts and bad news head-on. I have never known anyone, myself included, who enjoys conflicts. However, ignoring a conflict does not cause it to go away. In fact, it nourishes the disagreement and allows it to fester and become worse. That isn't good for anyone. **If something isn't working, face it head-on.** You are best to follow the ancient proverb and 'never leave a nail sticking up where you find it.'

"Along those same lines, when there is bad news, don't allow it to simmer until it eventually boils over. The best time to **address bad news is as quickly as you can**. Bad news rarely improves with age."

Jack couldn't resist commenting. "That's for sure. Ignoring issues and delaying bad news allows both to grow into ugly situations. I'm a witness."

Grace smiled and agreed. "I have ignored issues too. I hoped they would just disappear, but it never happened. But I forced myself to get into the habit of saying 'do something at once, do something at once, do something at once,' three or four times a day. It became an important reminder for me to keep moving forward and get things done. That revelation has made a huge difference in my life … it can make a difference in your life as well."

"I understand your emphasis on 'Do something at once,' but aren't there times when you need to *not* do something at once?" Jack questioned. "Or maybe wait?"

"You're one step ahead of me." Grace was pleased Jack was connecting with her lesson. "To be fair, there are a couple of times when it's best to wait. ***When you're angry is not the time to 'do something at once.'*** Wait until you can respond without anger. Walk away, take some deep breaths, gather your emotions before you address the issue that has outraged you. When you are emotionally threatened, it is not a good time to counter with emotional threats.

"An angry person does not think clearly. It is never a good idea to call someone or send an email or text when you are angry. Sleep on it and then tackle the situation when you can do it without anger. And it would be wise to talk the situation through with a mentor. Having an unbiased sounding board may prevent you from saying something you'll later regret.

"Another time to wait is ***when you're making a major decision.*** Any major decision should be analyzed thoroughly to understand the long-term consequences. All major financial and family decisions should be done slowly."

"Doesn't your suggestion to wait contradict attacking procrastination?" Jack added, attempting to reconcile a few things that bothered him.

"Remember, waiting does not contradict attacking procrastination in those cases because procrastination does not begin until you have enough facts to move forward," Grace reminded him. "If you have all the facts available and thoroughly understand the consequences of your decision, then you can move forward without further delay.

"One main reason I've been able to achieve success is because I am passionate about becoming my very best. I have found my passion for achievements in my life, and work has exposed me to all kinds of possibilities. I think the same can happen to you. Achieving success and happiness is a process that requires you to 'do something at once,' not just think about doing something. *Ask yourself: What is the best use of my time right now?* Then, get on with it. You need to keep moving forward, one step at a time, and go as far as you can see. When you get there, the next step will be obvious. You need to make the first move and get started right now."

Jack appreciated Grace's advice and wanted more. "Is there anything else you can share with me?"

"How many more people are you scheduled to talk to?" Grace asked.

"You are my final one," Jack answered. "My next step is to create my own success plan. However, I don't plan on this being the last time I talk with you, or any of the other people who have helped me. My desire is to develop a relationship with each of you and continue to learn from you."

"I think that's a good plan." Grace was encouraging. "When you began your journey, you were stuck and didn't know what to do. It reminds me of a story:

"Once there was a man walking down the street who fell into a hole. The hole was so deep he couldn't escape. He looked in all directions but couldn't figure out how to raise himself from the hole.

"A preacher walked by, heard the man's cry for help and inquired, 'Why are you in that hole in the road?' The man replied: 'I fell in and I can't get out.' The preacher said that he would pray for him and walked away.

"A police officer walked by, heard the man's cry for help and inquired, 'Why are you in that hole in the road?' The man replied: 'I fell in and I can't get out.' The policeman said it was against the law to be in a hole in the road, wrote him a ticket, threw it into the hole and walked away.

"An environmentalist walked by, heard the man's cry for help and inquired, 'Why are you in that hole in the road?' The man replied, 'I fell in and I can't get out.' The environmentalist said it was environmentally unsafe to be in a hole in the road and began to picket, circling the hole and holding a sign reading, 'Man in Hole in Road … Environmentally Unsafe!'

"A friend walked by, heard the man's cry for help and inquired, 'Why are you in that hole in the road?' The man replied, 'I fell in and I can't get out.' Without hesitation, the friend jumped into the hole with him.

"The man in the hole said, 'Are you crazy? Why did you jump in this hole? I've tried the best I can, but I can't find a way out. I have a preacher praying for me, a policeman writing me a ticket, and this goofy environmentalist picketing outside … and you chose to jump down here with me. Are you crazy? Why would you jump down here with me?'

"The friend replied, 'Don't worry. I chose to jump in this hole with you because I've been in this hole before and I know the way out!'

"You are the man in the hole," Grace explained. "All the people you have visited have jumped in the hole with you. Once you begin implementing your plan, it will be your turn to jump in the hole with someone else who doesn't know how to escape his or her situation.

"Whatever you have learned is not yours to keep. It's yours to pass on to others. I'm quite certain you, too, will learn something new when you teach others. It's called 'circular learning.' That's one of the beautiful things about mentoring – the coach learns as much as, or even more than the person who was being coached. Just as I have with you.

"One last thing. Life is too short not to be happy, and too long not to become the very best version of you. Start having fun. Keep your sense of humor and surround yourself with people who will lift you higher and who want to have fun as well. The successful people I know have enjoyed their journey. You can too."

"Thank you for coming to see me," Grace said as she stood up. "This time has been valuable to me. I hope that it's been just as valuable to you, and that you will 'do something at once' to begin seizing your moment."

"Your time and your insights have been incredibly valuable to me," Jack replied. "Thank you. Stopping procrastination and moving forward faster are habits I need to develop if I'm going to become the person I want to be."

Jack was again surprised by the simplicity of the advice he had just received. As he walked out to his car he thought to himself, *'Do something at once' … I wish I'd taken that advice many years ago. I own my time. I need to use it well.*

He had visited with some amazing individuals. All had offered advice and guidance he was eager to incorporate into his daily routine. Jack had been pleasantly surprised how kindly each of the mentors had treated him. He'd learned that he could be successful, confident, and likable at the same time.

Jack's journey was now complete. It was time for him to take everything he had learned and create his own success plan.

Grace's Lessons:

I do something at once. Procrastination is an enemy. I will never get ahead without getting started.

I will not respond when I am angry. I will cool down and carefully consider my response.

I own my time. It is up to me to make the best use of it.

Knowing I have something to do that I should have already done increases my stress.

Perfection may not be worth its price. Perfection paralysis is expensive.

Life is short. I need to start enjoying it.

From Jack Davis to Everyone

When Jack began creating his personal success plan, he reflected on some of the common traits of the successful people he visited along his journey. He wrote them down:

Each person had an "abundance" mentality. They were willing to share their knowledge without asking anything in return, and they weren't afraid to give away any "secrets." He learned that the biggest secret about success was that there was no secret. These successful people believed there is plenty of knowledge, wisdom and success for everyone. One person's achievements did not diminish the possibilities for anyone else; there was room for everyone to be successful. They were happy to help him without considering what they would receive in return.

Each of his mentors had been on a success journey of their own. They'd had challenges and weren't afraid to admit it. They were not gifted in every area of life, but they were willing to learn from other people who were better in these weak areas. They understood the power of their choices and learned to look into the future to see the consequences of the present choices they were making.

Even though they each had different talents and experiences, each person was dedicated to being his or her very best. They were not just interested in becoming their best, they were committed to making it happen. They had cultivated a great personal reputation by exhibiting positive action, discipline and energy.

The successful people worked hard. They did not work just to get paid. They were obsessed with making things better. It might have seemed that winning was easy for them, but winning only came after hard work.

They loved their work, and yet, they maintained balance in their lives. They learned how to integrate their careers into their lives. Their careers did not take priority over their family life. They each believed that achieving success at all costs was not success at all. They refused to sacrifice everything in the pursuit of career success. And they chose to invest their careers in something that engaged their hearts as well as their minds.

Each person had a healthy blend of humility and confidence. They were quick to acknowledge the impact of other people in their lives. They were grateful and readily gave credit to those who helped them along the way. They willingly shared their wisdom with confidence. They were swift to forgive themselves and others.

The room immediately lit up when each person walked in. They projected a positive image and their appearance reflected their success. They were polished, looked their best, dressed well and had a positive demeanor. They focused their attention on making others feel better about themselves. They asked questions and were genuinely interested in the answers. They were quick with a smile and encouragement.

Most importantly, though, **each of them understood the difference between existing and living**. They enjoy life because they live with purpose. They have a clear sense of direction and take positive actions daily that fulfill their purpose.

Through meeting with successful individuals, Jack discovered he *did*, indeed, have unique talents. His courage to ask for advice, his willingness to learn, and his enthusiasm for becoming the person he wanted to be were all valuable talents.

Jack's personal success plan became obvious. All his visits contributed to his plan.

He began to grasp that, no matter what happened to him, it was up to him to take responsibility to move forward into a better place. He accepted that change was essential to his success, and he could hug change instead of resisting it. He realized he had to know, without a doubt, his purpose and maintain his personal values above all else.

He became a student of his mistakes and learned to develop a 'never again' response to make sure he didn't repeat them. He learned to quit making up things he wanted to be true and begin saluting the truth. He became a man of his word. When he committed to something, you could consider it done. He also decided to be great in small things. He had to consciously improve his attitude if he was to become the person he wanted to be.

Jack became a curious person and asked *why* more often than he had in the past. This new trait gave him the confidence to realize that what he was doing was important enough to be done well.

He learned to live in peace. He forgave those who offended him, and he forgave himself.

He understood that the principles shared by his successful mentors were a wonderful gift. He was able to begin working diligently on a defined plan to become the person he wanted to be.

He got lucky when he began seeking knowledge. He read more and listened better. He was not afraid to take action and did something at once without procrastinating.

His marriage got back on track. He was able to balance the important things in his life and make dedicated time for his family a priority.

Jack became one of the most successful people in his community. He did not make the most money, live in the largest house or drive the finest car, but he learned that his success was about more than those things. It was about becoming *his* very best, enjoying life and helping others become the person they wanted to be.

He also became a great student of the lessons he had learned from the mentors in his town. He learned that accomplishing other people's perceptions of success was not as important as achieving his definition of success.

The most important thing Jack learned was the joy of sharing his knowledge with everyone. This is his gift to you.

Pass it on.

From the Author

Thank you for reading this book. I hope Jack's story will become part of your own success journey, as it has mine.

During my journey, I had to learn that, *regardless of what was happening in my life*, I was solely responsible for two things – my thoughts and my behavior. Once I accepted that fact and stopped blaming, making excuses and complaining, I was able to move forward.

I had to learn to '*hug change.*' Many things came relatively easy for me, so I did not see why I needed to change some things. This stubbornness held me back. It took me a while to overcome, but I have learned to appreciate the process of changing even when things are not yet broken. I hope it will be a good lesson for you, too.

Several times in my career, I was tempted to shortcut my core values to accomplish something important to me at the time. I learned there is no such thing as shortcutting values. You either live them, or you don't. For me to achieve long-term success, I had to '*quit drifting*' and live my values all day, every day.

Living the '*saluting the truth*' principle has saved me much time and misery. When my business was struggling, I learned quickly that I could not afford to make the same mistakes twice. In addition, while I was failing, several of my friends bailed on me. I had to forgive them in order to move on. I learned that harboring grudges would only hold me back and prevent me from moving forward.

I had to '*lift my own fog*' and recognize there was always something that could be done and something I could do. I learned it's difficult to be bogged down with worry as long as I'm diligently working toward improving a situation.

I learned people will drown you with good ideas if you just ask them. Part of my operating philosophy is to '*ask why*' frequently. I found my best answer to many questions was 'I don't know. What do you think?' Many wonderful, creative, ideas came from the people who were on the front line, ready to provide the answer to that question.

I am a living example that '*luck resides in knowledge.*' I discovered early in my career that if I learned more, I would be more valuable to those around me. I also learned that knowledge has to be nurtured and increased or it will vanish. You can get lucky and enjoy the power of knowledge. And, you can '*do something at once.*' Don't delay. You can take control, beginning right now.

As you can see, I have dropped in on all the mentors Jack visited in this book. I have been the recipient of wonderful, fruitful advice. My advice to you is to take what you have learned in this book and do two things:

1. **Apply each of these lessons beginning today.** Go back and review each chapter and develop an action plan. The key is to get started. You can get started today.

2. Teach these principles to others. The most effective way to learn is to teach; it will clarify your ideas and reinforce your own learning. You can lead a discussion group at work or in your community. You may want to teach those around your own dinner table as well. A free guide for small discussion group and reproducible handouts are available at www.CornerStoneLeadership.com to help you get started.

Don't sit on your knowledge – share it. When you lift other people up, they will lift you up.

As a younger man, one of my heroes was Payne Stewart, who won the U.S. Open Golf Championship in 1999. Shortly after that victory, he perished in a tragic airplane accident. Payne was a charismatic, fun-loving guy who had a passion for his work, combined with a deep faith in his purpose. Shortly before his death, he was quoted as saying: "The thing about dreams is sometimes you get to live them out."

That is how I feel about my career. I have lived out my dreams. One of my dreams is to encourage you and others to become your best in whatever dream you have chosen in your life.

What if you chose to take control of every aspect of your life? Imagine how you would feel arriving at work being thankful for your job and the people around you? How would you feel to be enthusiastic about your life? How would it feel to have renewed energy so you could spend more quality time with your loved ones? How would you feel to have a marriage filled with more intimacy, joy, honesty, and friendship? How would you feel to have control over your debt? How would you feel to be at peace with yourself and everyone around you?

I think you would feel magnificent.

You can make those choices. Life's greatest rewards often appear in unexpected places. Keep your eyes open, your faith intact, and search for those rewards. They are ready to be discovered.

My greatest desire is that the principles provided in *Destination: Success* will provide you encouragement and knowledge so you will make the decision to become the person you want to be.

The next move is always yours. This is your life, your time, and your opportunity.

May life's journey bring you happiness and success.

David Cottrell
Boerne, Texas

Acknowledgments

I have been one of the most fortunate people in the world because of my faith, family, friends, and associates. My success has been molded and formed by those whom I have been fortunate enough to be on the same team.

Thanks to my friends who have encouraged me and have taken the time to make me a part of their lives. I am especially grateful to Louis Kruger, Mark Layton, Tod Taylor, Bryan Lancaster, Bob Biddle, Arlen Espinal, and Paul Liberato.

Thanks to the CornerStone team: Barbara Bartlett, Ken Carnes, Lee Colan, Harry Hopkins, Kathleen Green, Michele Lucia, and Melissa Farr and our 20,000 customers who have remained loyal to CornerStone for the past 24 years. Please accept my deepest gratitude.

Thanks to Alice Adams, who taught me how to write over twenty years ago, and to Brenda Quinn, my editor, who provided wonderful spice and clarity to this book.

Thanks to Steve Williford and Bill Catlette, who both provided me professional direction; Ashley LeBlanc, who provided a fresh perspective on several of the chapters; Lee Colan, who introduced me to the say/do ratio ... you need to read his book, *Sticking to It*; Frank Lunn, who, in 2002 at a writer's conference in Los Angeles, taught me about Someday Isle; and David Cook, my long-time friend who taught me to See, Feel, and Trust. He authored one of my favorite books and movies of all time: ***Seven Days in Utopia: Golf's Sacred Journey.***

Special thanks to my wife Madeline who endured reading aloud with me at least six different versions of this book.

Without a doubt, I am one of the most fortunate people in the world. I thank God every day for allowing me the opportunity to live my dream.

To each person who reads this book, I hope that it will inspire you to your greatest success.

The Next Step – Implement
Destination: Success
into Your Organization

Destination: Success! **PowerPoint™ Presentation**

This cost-effective, downloadable PowerPoint™ presentation includes a professionally prepared PowerPoint™ deck, detailed facilitator guide, notes and license for unlimited reproduction of participant guides for your internal company use. $149

Visit www.CornerStoneLeadership.com

Keynote Presentation

Invite author David Cottrell to inspire your team and help create greater success for your organization. Contact Michele@DavidCottrell.com

 Destination: Success! **Reproducible Handouts**
You can lead your discussion group at work, home, school, or church through *Destination: Success!* with our free, five session, small group guide and reproducible handouts.

You do not have to be an expert in success or facilitation to lead your group. The FREE small group guide provides everything you need.

Download at www.CornerStoneLeadership.com.

Time Management Assessment and Goal Setting Process Worksheet
Download at www.CornerStoneLeadership.com.

Destination: Success!

Quantity Discounts:

1-30 copies	$19.95
31-100 copies	$17.95
100+ copies	$14.95

www.CornerStoneLeadership.com

The *Destination: Success!* Package

Includes all 10 books pictured for
only $109.95!

(A savings of over 30%)

For additional leadership resources,
visit **www.CornerStoneLeadership.com**

Thank you for reading
Destination: Success!

We hope it has assisted you in your quest
for personal and professional growth.
CornerStone Leadership's mission is to
fuel knowledge with practical resources
that will accelerate your success and life satisfaction!

CornerStone
Leadership Institute

www.**CornerStoneLeadership**.com